The Dopamine Connection

Maximize Your Potential With Sleep, Nutrition, and Brain Health

Ameri Dacre

Table of Contents

Introduction

The relationship between dopamine and overall well-being is gaining prominence in modern life as the frenetic scenario exacerbates dopamine production in the human brain. Recent years have witnessed a rise in chronic diseases and mental health problems, revealing the side effects of our digital and technological age. Thus, it's necessary to comprehend the neurotransmitter of reward and pleasure in the brain to have a holistic understanding of well-being.

A lifestyle unlike any other has emerged in the wake of the modern era's whirlwind of progress, where technological marvels intertwine us globally. Still, as we adapt to these advances, an undeniable paradox has developed with consequences for our health. We now look into dopamine and its significance in understanding this issue.

The present setting relies on two significant factors: dopamine and the contemporary way of living. It functions as the essential element of the brain that deals with incentive, satisfaction, and enthusiasm stimulation. But as society evolved, it glamorized the instant gratification culture and the concept of always chasing after rewards. To achieve comprehensive awareness, these two vital components must intertwine. An atmosphere prevails where dopamine-releasing stimuli confront more individuals each day, be it through food delivery apps or social media. This can trigger the onset of an addiction where an individual's ceaseless endeavor to feel good leads to a state of emotional and mental fatigue.

An unsettling analysis of mental health data uncovers a worrisome truth. Globally, over 300 million people are affected by anxiety disorders, while depression is the primary cause of disability, affecting over 280 million individuals as per the World Health Organization (2017, 2022). These statistics provide a stark reminder of how the constant pursuit of dopamine can negatively impact our mental well-being. The overstimulation of this neurotransmitter can provoke depression, anxiety, and even more severe maladies.

Gazing intently into the current way of life, it becomes apparent that we are ensnared in an unceasing loop. Social media, constructed to be attractive and captivating, manifests itself as the quintessential exemplar of how prodigious levels of dopamine can be cunning. Each moment we find ourselves in the never-ending "feed" scrolling through, an influx of dopamine engulfs the brain, imparting a momentary sense of contentment. Yet, this fleeting gratification eventually dissipates, leaving behind a sense of vacuity, and pushing us to devote more time on these platforms in the pursuit of the next "hit" of euphoria.

Maintaining balance in our lives stands out as a fundamental point when unraveling the correlation between dopamine production and mental health. The negative consequences of the constant pursuit of dopamine can be offset by maintaining a healthy lifestyle that encompasses stress management practices, regular exercise, and a balanced diet. Exercise, in particular, releases endorphins, a different type of neurotransmitter, that not only generates good feelings but also regulates dopamine levels in the brain.

Mindfulness and self-discipline play a vital role in preventing the harmful effects of dopamine seeking. It's worth noting that not all aspects of seeking dopamine are damaging. Actually, dopamine seeking is an essential component of one's biology and can inspire us to reach our objectives and feel genuine happiness. Nevertheless, an unhealthy cycle of seeking can adversely impact our well-being, both mentally and physically.

With the normalization of instant gratification, cultivating the skill of delaying it and finding fulfillment in meaningful undertakings becomes paramount. The reorientation of our dopamine connection can be achieved through mindfulness and meditation practices. By promoting present-moment attention, these practices reduce the urge to seek perpetual gratification while enabling a mindful focus on our emotions and actions.

In order to tackle this issue in a meaningful way, we must adopt both individual and societal tactics. First, understanding the role of dopamine production on our actions and feelings to make personal changes. We should actively avoid instant gratification patterns and prioritize actions that promote long-term happiness. On a larger scale, we need to challenge and modify structures that prioritize financial gain over healthy dopamine levels. This means rethinking the ways we create and utilize products and technology.

Modern Lifestyle Accommodations

Throughout history, human lifestyles have been drastically altered by time's thread, creating a unique tapestry. The present-day is a bustling era brimming with advancements in technology and culture, bringing both conveniences and challenges. The fast-paced, interconnected lifestyle has resulted in significant changes directly affecting physical and psychological well-being. It's essential to recognize the complex physiological mechanisms governing our lives and the repercussions of these changes, including how dopamine affects our bodies. As we navigate through this transformative era, comprehension and mindfulness are vital.

Today's lifestyle is a jumble of stimuli and demands. We can't seem to escape technology as it blends together with our communication, work, and entertainment. Information is at our fingertips, thanks to mobile devices and social networks. However, the web's connection is relentless, creating a perpetual state of being connected. Curiously, whilst this global accessibility has fostered greater interaction, it has also paradoxically brought about feelings of loneliness and seclusion. The more we connect, the more we seem to feel disconnected.

The human psyche has undergone a transformation in the midst of the digital turmoil that defines modern existence. A consequence of being overwhelmed is "attention fatigue," which makes it tough to concentrate on tasks and breeds negative feelings, including anxiety and dissatisfaction. Social media exacerbates the problem with curated accounts showcasing unattainable perfection, inducing personal inadequacy and worsening mental health.

With the dawn of modern times, physical activity has assumed a fresh appearance. Everyday tasks that were once mundane have been partially mechanized, making our lifestyles exceedingly convenient. This has resulted in a more straightforward mode of transport due to automobiles, eliminating the need for unnecessary walking. Nonetheless, the progress that modernization has bestowed on us, although exceptional, has had its share of health-related complications. Modern advancements have brought about new challenges, even as they've eased physical burdens. One significant disadvantage of reduced physical activity is its link to numerous diseases, including obesity and cardiovascular conditions.

In the intertwined web of health and modernity, dopamine rises as a pivotal component. This neurotransmitter is crucial in dictating motivation, enjoyment, and compensation. Serving as the "chemical messenger," dopamine induces the reward mechanism in the brain, which provides a feeling of contentment and fulfillment when we indulge in enjoyable things. In modern society, dopamine takes on added significance since numerous current pursuits are intended to trigger its release.

Generating "likes," comments, and notifications via technology and social networks is intended to produce small doses of dopamine. Our brains release a dopamine rush when we receive a notification on our phone, driving us to examine and answer it. This chain of rewards helps reinforce how we use our devices and leads us into a digital interaction spiral. Unfortunately, this over-stimulation can cause damage to our mental well-being.

The issue at hand is the mishandling of the reward system. If there is a continuous bombardment of triggers that instigate dopamine discharge, the mind may adapt to it and become desensitized. Consequently, this makes it necessary for there to be an increase in the magnitude of such stimuli to generate the same level of contentment, which might bring about compulsive tendencies and an ongoing quest for fulfillment. Essentially, acclimatizing to unceasing digital provocations can alter one's perception of contentment and joy in other domains of life, and result in the deterioration of one's mental well-being.

The ability to postpone gratification is undermined in a society that heavily relies on instant rewards, and dopamine plays a role in both decision-making and motivation. While it's important to set and strive for long-term goals, dopamine sometimes convinces us to prioritize immediate rewards instead. As a result, our productivity and perseverance can suffer, making it challenging to accomplish truly meaningful objectives.

Fostering a sense of equilibrium amidst the strain of modern life is important for preserving our mental and physical well-being. Initially, we need to acknowledge the influence of technology and other contemporary modifications on our health. Restricting our use of electronic devices, embracing mindfulness, and cultivating genuine real-life relationships are tactics that can help combat the detrimental repercussions of excessive digital exposure.

Our comprehension of dopamine and its function offers insight into better emotional and behavioral management. Rather than relying solely on external stimuli for pleasure, we can develop practices that encourage healthy dopamine release—like routine exercise, creative endeavors, and setting fulfilling objectives. By knowing that dopamine isn't a mere reward mechanism but a molecule that affects various cognitive and emotional processes, we are better equipped to make informed choices about our relationship with the world around us.

As a key player in the interplay, dopamine not only directs the creation of pleasurable feelings and contentment, but also affects our drive, our choices, and our habits' development. Its interactions with the digital landscape and immediate rewards must be acknowledged and regulated accordingly. Rather than being propelled by ceaseless striving for immediate satisfaction, we can utilize thoughtful tactics to harmonize our undertakings and focuses.

In order to combat the negative consequences of modernization, fostering self-discipline is a vital tactic. In a world overflowing with diversions, the power to set limits and concentrate on significant duties functions as a foundation for upholding sound mental health. Self-discipline encompasses the ability to quell the urge to repeatedly check one's phone, to refrain from indulging in excessive digital entertainment, and to give precedence to moments of introspection and self-nurturing.

In this modern epoch, mindfulness has surged in relevancy. It entails being intentionally present in the moment, void of judgments, or being swayed by one's thoughts or diversions. This practice offers potential benefits such as lowered anxiety and stress, heightened focus, and a fuller engagement with the fluctuations of ordinary existence. By simply divvying up moments to genuinely tune into our breath and surroundings, a sense of composure can be fostered amid the confused pace of contemporary life.

Prioritizing authentic and genuine human relationships is crucial. Even with virtual connectivity, meaningful face-to-face interactions remain essential. Investing in personal connections can act as a safeguard against the harmful impacts of loneliness and solitude. Cultivating emotional support, conversing, and sharing experiences can holistically aid our mental and emotional well-being.

The importance of stimulating physical activity cannot be overemphasized. Our current era teems with gadgets and services that make movement less necessary, but we must resist using this as a pretext to not take action. Exercise routines should thus be infused into our daily lives, given the positive effects they have on both cardiovascular and mental well-being. As we exercise, endorphins are released, these being the neurotransmitters responsible for inducing feelings of pleasure and reducing tension.

Reclaiming authority over our mental and physical health involves comprehending the effects of dopamine on our existence, a lesson that can pack quite a punch. By being informed about how dopamine release is shaped by current stimuli and our behavioral patterns, we're able to make intentional and informed choices. This ensures that we control our habits and activities rather than being ruled by them. Ultimately, this allows us to recapture a measure of control over our mental and physical well-being.

The process of adapting to modern living is ever-changing and requires a thorough comprehension of its effects on our mental and physical health. Embracing modern society enables both positive and negative outcomes, and the critical factor is finding an equilibrium where technology can benefit us without harming our well-being. The chemical compound, dopamine, is a key element in this dynamic and brings to mind the warnings of addiction and mental health consequences that may arise from instant gratification. By developing self-control, engaging in mindfulness, establishing authentic human relationships, and pursuing healthy physical activity habits, we can effectively navigate the complex labyrinth of modernity.

In the dialogue about Dopamine dysregulation wreaking havoc in our contemporary way of life, a refreshing outlook emerges—you have the potential to assert significant authority over your situation. To attain a beneficial dopamine equilibrium, being intuitive and inculcating a daily healthy habit is paramount. You can seize hold of your virtual engagements, limit screen time, thus reducing constant sensory stimulation, and create recuperative breathing space. Incorporating meditation, exercise, and real human connections into our lives can assist in countering the negative effects of immediate satisfaction. Enhancing our relationships with ourselves and others by engaging in genuine experiences has the power to empower us to take charge of our emotional and mental state in today's world of overwhelming dopamine stimuli. Later in these pages, we will go over the most effective tactics for balance when we find ourselves trapped in the technological environment. But first, we will learn about all the systems and functions dopamine is responsible for in our body. This sense of knowledge will help you apply and be inspired to practice the exercises displayed.

Chapter 1:

The Role of Dopamine

Our being is epitomized by a complex process—a neurological coordination initiated by brain communication. The intricate process involves specialized cells of the nervous system known as neurons interweaving information in a dynamic process, where electrical and chemical signals come together to create a beautiful choreography that governs multiple bodily and mental functions. This process is all-encompassing and accompanies us from basic movements to deep emotional and twisted cognitive considerations.

Two primary factors are essential for brain communication: electrical and chemical signals. Electrical flashes that transmute into neural networks permit lightning-fast information flow over short distances. In contrast, chemical signals come into play through the discharge of specific molecules called neurotransmitters. These molecules are released at neuronal interactions, also known as synapses, and activate receptors on neighboring neurons. This interweaving transmission along the neuronal weft creates chemical messengers.

The corridors of the brain, neurons, utilize special molecules—neurotransmitters—to transmit information to each other. These message carriers are expelled by a neuron into a synapse, which is a tiny space connecting the neurons sending the message with the neurons receiving the message. This is where the exciting part occurs: as an electric impulse leaves the neuron, the neurotransmitters are set free into the synaptic space. The brain works like a communication network, with neurotransmitters serving as the email equivalent for message delivery.

The receiving neuron reacts to a perfect lock and key that opens up a specific junction between the two. The response that follows can either be a signal to inhibit communication or an electrical signal that encourages it.

Branching through every experience we have, this cerebral communication holds great importance. Whether it's the slightest motor gestures like moving a finger or larger cognitive endeavors like solving puzzles or expressing emotions, all of it originates from this elaborate neural exchange. On the brain's grand stage, neural networks come together like combined pieces, entwining neurons into complex designs that facilitate a seamless transfer of information through specific avenues.

In a wondrous fashion, the neuron's wiring does not limit itself to the boundaries of the brain. Instead, it spreads to other regions of the nervous system, including the spinal cord and peripheral nerves. This web links the body as a whole, connecting to the brain and spinal cord with masterful coordination. Consequently, multiple functions and behaviors arise, allowing the organism to stand as one cooperative entity, even in an ever-changing environment.

Emotions and desires are governed by a chemical called dopamine, which has the added capability of reaching outside of the brain to affect motor control. The maintenance of smooth and consistent movements within the black substance pathways in the brain is highly dependent on dopamine. If this component is absent, it can lead to the onset of degenerative diseases such as Parkinson's, causing a jolt to the once-sleek neuronal activity.

Operating as a conductor in the complex process of human biology, dopamine is a fascinating particle. This essential neurotransmitter impacts numerous vital functions and serves as a lead, orchestrating the biochemical symphony. While it's famous for incentivizing, satiating, and gratifying, dopamine's influence surpasses its psychological impact. It happily intermingles with physiological mechanisms and pervades all the nooks and crannies of our anatomy at the cellular level.

The central nervous system's communication network relies on dopamine, the primary chemical messenger. In specific brain areas responsible for motor control and the reward system, dopamine triggers electrical signals between neurons at synapses, facilitating information transmission, as we explained previously in more detail. In other words, dopamine acts as a mediator, enabling optimal brain communication.

Dopamine reigns in the reward system—a heaven for education and pleasure in the center of its fame. It cascades upon us when we encounter satisfying circumstances, inducing euphoria and satisfaction. The goal-oriented missions we conquer or even a single sip of coffee in the morning are sufficient to stimulate dopamine and push us forward.

Certain actions signal the brain and trigger reward signals, which help strengthen the connection between various stimuli and positive outcomes, providing us with associative learning. Behaviors that bring us satisfaction become habitual, as a result of this conditioning process. Dopamine plays a big part in this neural activity.

An overabundance of dopamine, like that seen in some cases of schizophrenia, can be detrimental to cognitive function. Its overexcitement can cause a breakdown of delicate processes and expose inconsistencies in reality. Hallucinations and delusions can interrupt the natural order when dopamine levels get out of hand, proving biochemical harmony is paramount.

Always present in our lives, with its complexity and dynamism, dopamine amazes us in its ingrained influence in every nook and cranny of our being. This versatile chemical messenger shapes our passions and aspirations while managing electrical impulses that traverse our enigmatic brain. Movement and emotion's juxtaposition to motivation's peak are all influenced by this neurotransmitter.

Regulation of Dopamine Levels

The delicate process of regulating dopamine levels in the brain is a fascinating aspect of neurophysiology. This chemical messenger is a component of the brain, providing it with unparalleled energy. However, unbridled dopamine levels can also cause an unhealthy imbalance, making its management a huge challenge.

A variety of techniques are utilized by the brain to manage overwhelming doses of dopamine and maintain self-discipline. One of the key contenders in this battle is the negative feedback mechanism, a virtuous loop that dampens dopamine emissions when they climb too high. This coordination is facilitated by specific dopamine receptors that communicate to the brain when overstimulation ensues, prompting it to reduce dopamine production.

In response to signals, neurons demonstrate constant adaptation and exhibit resilient brain plasticity, which is defined in simple words as a malleable and transformative capacity of neural networks to function as stimulation and learning. As a safeguard, dopamine receptors' density and sensitivity in the reward system are adjusted through down-regulation. This is performed to maintain delicate harmony in the brain levels of dopamine.

The serotonergic system, which is the system that regulates serotonin production, is a valuable ally when the dopamine levels are too high. It works to keep emotions in check and maintain balance in the brain. Serotonin competes with dopamine for neural resources and uses its calming abilities to help maintain steady emotions.

Guarding the flood of dopamine is the prefrontal cortex, known for its executive prowess. With its vigilant supervision and calculated restraint, this critical center tempers the fervent impulses that subcortical circuits may generate. This harmonious waltz of instinct and judgment grants the brain the ability to curb the overwhelming effects of hyperdopaminergia.

The regulation of dopamine levels in the brain is a wondrous display of natural adaptability and equilibrium. With its negative feedback system, attenuated by serotonin and overseen by the prefrontal cortex, the brain conducts a biochemical concert to sustain functional and emotional balance at the neurological crossroads. It's truly a neural ballet, as we will continue to see.

Dopamine's Interaction With Other Neurotransmitters

Interacting molecules in our brains affect our emotions and actions in an entrancing way. Achieving the spotlight in this neural network are two prominent neurotransmitters—dopamine and serotonin—who perform a magnificent duet, as we have seen. Dopamine supplies the motivation and reaps the rewards, while serotonin regulates our emotions, as previously explained. Together, they leave an indelible impression not only on our mindset but also on our conduct. More neurotransmitters are involved in this network connected to the dopamine molecule.

An extraordinary partnership exists between dopamine and norepinephrine that has unique effects. Norepinephrine, also known as noradrenaline, supports heightened alertness and concentration, priming us for challenges. It works alongside dopamine to create an exceptional balance of stress response regulation and attention management. With delicate chemicals in the central nervous system, their collaboration yields a remarkable and subtle pattern of activation and adaptation.

The plot that shapes our daily experience is a result of the constant and unpredictable cross-interaction between various neurotransmitter systems. The serotonergic, dopaminergic, and noradrenergic systems, all vying for dominance, create both synergistic and competitive reactions, which in turn cause unforeseen results.

Emotions are complex and have layered pathways. The modulation of neuropeptide release is crucial to dopamine's effects. Social bonding, response to stress, and pain perception can all be influenced based on the neurochemical balance of neurotransmitter systems. Dopamine's effects rely heavily on its interactions with substance P and oxytocin.

The neural circuits involved in forming emotional memories and learning require communication between the dopamine and glutamate systems. Neural adaptation and synaptic plasticity previously reviewed rely specifically on the synergistic interaction of glutamate, the dominant excitatory neurotransmitter in the brain, with dopamine.

In summary, our psyche is a byproduct of a singular chemical perfect coordination happening inside our head. The interconnections and interactions between diverse neurotransmitters, with a particular focus on dopamine, significantly impact our experiences and actions. Among the many molecular unions that mold our psyche is the graceful and principal camaraderie of serotonin with dopamine and the energetic fusion of norepinephrine with dopamine.

Neuroplasticity

Dopamine is the player in the brain's fundamental characteristic of neuroplasticity. Nature involves this fascinating trait, which enables the brain to adapt and change constantly according to the information received.

The synaptic world buzzes with the power of dopamine, whose influence on the strength and plasticity of neuron connections is fundamental. Enhancing communication and shaping synapses, dopamine is a master of the brain's ability to alter connections based on the environment or experience, which is called synaptic plasticity. Every time you learn something new, your brain is chemically and physically modified.

Pursuing knowledge and modifying behavior is a realm where the correlation between synaptic plasticity and dopamine is present. The craving to explore new knowledge is driven by the dopamine-generated positive feedback in our brains. The release of dopamine extrudes a sense of gratification, which strengthens the neural connections we need for learning and cognitive functions. This, in turn, weaves any new information into our cognitive framework with greater delicacy.

The interplay of synaptic plasticity and dopamine is fundamental in shaping habits and adjusting behavior. Our brain releases dopamine when we engage in activities that yield satisfying outcomes, such as practicing a hobby or indulging in a tasty meal, which reinforces the brain's neural pathways responsible for those activities. Over time, this association between positive behavior and reward strengthens, forming long-lasting ingrained patterns. However, the same synaptic plasticity that creates these patterns can also have undesirable effects when negative or addictive experiences reprogram the reward circuits, perpetuating unwanted behavior.

Our emotional and cognitive faculties depend upon the complex dynamics of dopamine and synaptic plasticity in the human brain. The interplay between these factors contributes to our behavioral and learning adaptations, a testament to the brain's remarkable sophistication. Understanding the impact of our environment and actions on neural plasticity is important for cultivating beneficial habits and avoiding harmful ones. It is important to appreciate this equilibrium to foster healthy routines instead of succumbing to negative ones.

Motivation for a Thriving Life

This molecule dopamine plays a role in the complex realm of neurological activity by guiding and propelling us toward our objectives. It fascinates us with its governing abilities, conducting cellular activities that influence our urge to pursue and accomplish our desires.

Dopamine stands tall as the main figure in the sphere of motivation. It surges in areas of the brain connected to accomplishment or endeavors, kindling a feeling of excitement and satisfaction. This chemical response then morphs into the impetus behind our resolve to push ourselves past obstacles in order to achieve our dreams. Dopamine acts as a conductor, coordinating a harmony of actions to pursuit, fostering a sense of contentment upon reaching milestones or edging toward a sought-after aim.

Neurological issues can disrupt the connection between dopamine and motivation. This loss of drive can be caused by various factors, such as depression and Parkinson's disease. As a result of the imbalance of neurotransmitters, a lack of interest in activities that were once enjoyable can occur. It's almost as if the motivational soundtrack is drowned out in the midst of neural turmoil.

As we make our way through life, dopamine acts as the chief motivator, fueling our desire for success and recognition. Our tenacity and enthusiasm hinge on the proper flow and presence of this neurotransmitter. Yet, when things go awry, dopamine's influence can wane, resulting in a sense of desolation and detachment. Between motivation and dopamine illustrates the complex workings of our brains as we strive toward our greatest ambitions and the illusions that move us through life.

Chapter 2:

Dopamine's Effects on Mental

Health

With a mixture of feelings, this molecule manages pleasure and curiosity as well. Dopamine takes center stage, leading the way to new experiences and emotional rewards. Injecting vibrant notes into the brain's reward system, this molecule inspires unrelenting ambition and fuels a quest for satisfaction. Its tunes can inspire persistence and color life with hues of contentment.

Generating emotional alerts and assessing context, dopamine also acts as an internal critic. It stimulates executive function, encouraging concentration while adjusting mental focus based on relevance. Despite its benefits, it can also become hypercritical and cause anxiety and rumination. This hyper-reaction leads to drastic interpretations of stressful situations, which can create chronic worry.

Flexing its memory muscles, dopamine is responsible for knowledge and remarkable experiences. This molecule imbues memory with a rich tapestry of meaning, sealing moments of joy and pain into the space of the mind. Bleeding into the psyche, dopamine lends a cutting edge to psychology, allowing one to learn and adapt along the way.

In schizophrenia, the complex and challenging traces of dopamine create a discordant process that distorts reality, triggering hallucinations and delusions. On the other end of the spectrum, depression is intertwined with decreased dopamine release, drenching the psyche in shades of gray: disinterest and apathy.

In the psychological stage, dopamine plays a multifaceted role in mental health. It has both beneficial and challenging impacts on the brain that allow for progression and exploration. By comprehending its diverse functions, we can foster a strong and dynamic psychology that is adaptable to change.

Rewiring the brain to create emotional responses, opportunistic regulations involving gratification, motivation, and reward formation are carried out by a chemical messenger of the mind by the hand of the consciousness. This compound is responsible for creating pathways in the mind that help in the modulation of mood and transform external stimuli into a sensory experience.

Melancholy and euphoria are two emotional responses that add color to our inner experience, making mood regulation a complex and multidimensional process. The balancing act between these emotions is driven by several processes, creating a delicate experience within ourselves.

The power of perception and personal choice come into play when it comes to dopamine release through our psychological lens. The intertwining of events and their interpretations trigger a chain reaction of chemicals. Our mind possesses the power of focus and adaptation and thus plays a role in the regulation of our emotions. This syncretism ultimately puts the mind in a position of power.

Amidst the turmoil of emotions, self-regulation works as a guiding point. Harnessing emotional intelligence and compassionately examining the thoughts that fuel our feelings while practicing mindfulness, stabilizes the mind's navigation through rough waters. The synergy between neurobiological processes and cognitive abilities fuels our ability to manage our emotions with careful attention.

Our psychology and dopamine collide in a neural network full of biochemical signals and neurotransmitters. The psychological symptoms are the external expression and results of the combined chemical reactions in the brain. The synergy of our mind's agility and the complexity of the signals is vital at this juncture. Our regulation of moods is not passive and always changing. Conscious effort and understanding merge to sway the tide of emotions.

Amidst the inner workings of the human psyche, are performed by dopamine and the mind. This collaboration goes beyond mere biology, revealing how mood regulation is a constant source of fascination. The interplay between brain chemistry and conscious perception weaves a picture that steers our lives.

Social dynamics, skillfully influenced by dopamine, transform into an emotional relationship that crosses individual boundaries. When we interact with others, dopamine levels can rise, catalyzing a sense of connection and generating positive reinforcement toward the presence of certain individuals in our environment. This chemical and psychological amalgam molds the way we interpret others, shaping the affinities and antagonisms that underlie our social relationships.

The creation of emotional bonds, that delicate connection that binds people together in a web of trust and understanding, finds in dopamine a remarkably influential accomplice. At the base of the formation of lasting bonds, the release of dopamine in response to shared moments and pleasant experiences acts like a chisel, sculpting trust and empathy. These chemical flashes sow the seeds of emotional memories that ignite the embers of community and complicity.

However, this social element that dopamine helps to create is not one-dimensional. It can also fan the flames of competition and the quest for recognition, prompting people to engage in interactions where success and attention trigger the release of this prized neurochemical. In this way, dopamine becomes a driver of motivation, both toward bonding, self-improvement, and the construction of a social identity.

Dopamine is like an invisible storyteller, spinning the fibers of our psychology and the complexity of our social relationships into a deep and passionate narrative. From fleeting flashes of shared pleasure to emotional bonds that endure over time, its role in creating social interactions and bonds is inescapable. At the crossroads of brain chemistry and human interaction, dopamine stands as a vital link, a masterpiece in the ever-evolving mosaic of human experience.

When the curtain falls on insufficient production of this molecule, emotional and cognitive functioning is significantly affected, generating a domino effect that reverberates throughout daily life.

That is, when the levels of this substance fall below the appropriate thresholds, the tones of experience change. One of the most noticeable consequences is anhedonia, a gray blanket that covers the ability to experience pleasure in everyday activities. Passions that once illuminated life with vividness can become dull, creating a challenge to find satisfaction in even the simplest things.

Insufficient dopamine production can also manifest as a foggy cognitive clarity. Difficulty concentrating, planning, and making decisions becomes a constant challenge. The feeling that the mind is running at a slower speed can undermine confidence in intellectual abilities and weaken self-esteem. Obstacles seem higher and solutions more elusive, turning routine tasks into mountains that seem insurmountable.

The effects of dopamine depletion are not limited to the internal; they also trigger ripples in the social realm. Lack of energy and motivation can lead to social isolation, as interactions with others lose the sparkle and energy they used to have. Emotional bonds can blur as the ability to experience the pleasure of company is reduced, creating a cycle in which lack of social interaction perpetuates dopamine depletion.

The daily impact of insufficient dopamine production is a subtle path between sadness and frustration. Emotional and cognitive dullness can cloud perspective, creating a dark fog that seems to separate the individual from the world around them. However, it is important to remember that psychology and medicine are constantly evolving, offering therapeutic and pharmacological approaches that can restore adequate dopamine levels and restore nuance and vitality to daily life.

On the other hand, when this protagonist takes center stage with excessive production, the day-to-day narrative takes on a dizzying and often tumultuous pace.

Dopamine can reveal its fearless side when its levels exceed limits. In this scenario, symptoms manifest as dazzling flashes on the emotional horizon. Inordinate euphoria can become the main mood theme, leading to a feeling of constant ebullience. This dopamine hyperactivity can lead to a state of mania, where ideas flow at astonishing speed and confidence soars, often crossing the boundaries of reality.

Abrupt changes in brain chemistry can also generate an emotional roller coaster. Excitement can give way to irritability and emotional explosion, leading to a cycle of ups and downs that affect relationships and the ability to maintain a steady focus on tasks. The feeling that emotions are being tossed from one extreme to another can create a volatile emotional environment, where calmness seems unattainable.

In addition, excessive dopamine production can ignite the relentless pursuit of immediate gratification. Impulsivity and the tendency to take risks can increase, leading to rash decisions and reckless behavior. This urge to seek instant reward can lead to overstimulation and a sense of constant exhaustion as the body and mind struggle to keep up with the frantic pace.

Ultimately, excessive dopamine production stages a complex and often overwhelming emotional drama on a day-to-day basis. Oscillating between intense emotional states and the constant search for stimulation can create a whirlwind that affects both emotional stability and cognitive clarity.

Creativity Related to Dopamine Levels

Creativity is an exceptionally rich phenomenon. Dopamine, that chemical messenger that injects vitality into our experiences, plays a significant role in the genesis of imagination and artistic expression.

That river of fluid and atypical thoughts that flows in creative minds finds in dopamine a hidden muse. This molecule awakens the curls of ideas that distinguish the creative mind. The correlation between dopamine and creativity is like a constantly moving loom, where the threads of the molecule interconnect the corners of the imagination, giving them life and color.

The dynamic relationship between dopamine and creativity is such that, when released in response to rewarding situations, its presence also expands the wings of innovation and exploration. When dopamine flows, environments conducive to divergent thinking are generated, where unusual connections and fresh perspectives converge to shape new ideas and forms of expression. This relationship not only stimulates creativity but also plays an important role in the development of creative self-confidence.

However, the complexity of this relationship is not linear. While dopamine is an ally in creative generation, an excess of its presence can lead to overstimulation and loss of focus. Dopaminergic hyperactivity can generate distractions and abrupt jumps between ideas, making it difficult to channel and develop coherent creative projects. A careful balance between stimulation and regulation is essential to keep the spark of creativity from burning out of control.

In essence, dopamine and creativity establish a bond of interdependence on the stage of the human mind. Like a duet in a ceaseless waltz, they stimulate imagination and artistic expression with infectious energy. Maintaining a balance in this relationship is the key to unlocking the door to a world enriched by color and creative vitality, where the nuances of dopamine and the strokes of creativity converge to paint an inner masterpiece.

Debunking Myths About Anxiety and Dopamine

Anxiety disorders are associated with dopamine, the chemical that fuels incessant unease. Alongside ancestral fight or flight mechanisms, dopamine is linked to stress response. Previously, serotonin was the focus of anxiety regulation, but now dopamine is being recognized as a secondary player, influencing how the organism handles stress through the reward system.

The body and mind's response to stress heavily relies on the amount of dopamine released, which can lead to a fleeting feeling of joy mingling with the worries that anxiety brings about. As a result, the need for survival becomes sated by the search for pleasure, oscillating the balance between fighting back or fleeing from a situation that demands a response.

In neuroscience, the regulation of anxiety is a fascinating subject as it involves the interaction of various neurotransmitters, including dopamine. The dynamic interplay between these chemical messengers is a cross-disciplinary connection. Serotonin, which is commonly linked to emotional stability and calmness, cross-influences with dopamine in the balance. When there is an imbalance in these systems, altered anxiety and depression are evident, highlighting the interconnectedness of these molecules in mental health.

Anxiety remains a complex area for dopamine as it continues to puzzle researchers. When it's let loose, it can help provide relief from the symptoms, but at the same time, it can also cause further anxiety by stimulating the feeling of restlessness and pressure. Luckily, grasping this affiliation is fundamental when it comes to creating better ways of dealing with emotional regulation that consider the roles dopamine plays.

Concentration and Attention

Harmonic levels of dopamine in our brain are intertwined with our ability to connect with what's happening around us and understand the context. A proper balance of this molecule can allow us to direct our attention toward relevant goals and stimuli while suppressing distracting clutter.

When dopamine levels are aligned, a sustained concentration function is created. Our mind prepares to receive the most crucial instructions for the knowledge and tasks at hand. Neural circuits, groomed by dopamine, interlock so that distraction recedes, and the task's prominence rises.

Dopamine not only keeps us in the flow of a task but also supplies us with small doses of satisfaction as we move forward. Each achievement, each milestone reached, triggers a shower of chemical applause, reinforcing dedication and fueling persistence.

However, too much dopamine can unbalance concentration. Overstimulation can lead to detrimental hyperfocus, where we lose ourselves in trivial details or find ourselves unable to look away from the superficial. This out-of-tune spectacle can divert us from the real task at hand.

Optimism and Empowerment

On the other hand, dopamine not only reflects the search for tangible rewards but also awakens the song of optimism. As this substance floods the synapses, it creates a spectrum of sensations that glow like the rays of the rising sun. Anticipation of the rewards to come kindles a light of hope, with a psychological horizon where positive possibilities shine brightly.

Dopamine, in its role as an intrinsic motivator, creates a psychic foundation that fosters determination and a yearning for achievement. The sensation of overcoming obstacles and overcoming challenges becomes an internal wellspring of gratification, driving a virtuous cycle of action and satisfaction. Like a brain alchemist, dopamine transforms struggle into triumph, and each step forward feels like a miniature victory.

This chemistry of optimism and motivation possesses the power to recalibrate our attitude toward challenges. When dopamine leads the chorus, problems become opportunities, difficulties become exciting challenges. Fear of failure gives way to the desire to explore and learn. Even in the face of uncertainty, dopamine instills a tenacious spirit that refuses to give up.

However, as in any concept, balance is key. Dopamine, if deployed to excess, can lead us into the abyss of overstimulation. Overactive optimism can overshadow reality, and motivation can become an obsession. This is where the mastery lies in tuning dopamine sensibly, allowing energy and drive to flow smoothly.

An internal narrative guides us from the brink of exertion to a peak of self-validation, lit up by dopamine as a creator of individual potency. This architect of emotions refines our sense of achievement, imbuing it with a distinct liveliness.

A spectacle of empowerment arises when the neural gears release dopamine after achieving personal goals. This results in an inner glow that reignites self-efficacy and self-confidence. Each victory resonates within us, serving to remind us of our ability to shape our own destiny.

Self-development is a product of empowerment that's not just a temporary high. This is reflected in one's self-image as dopamine takes over the neural pathways. We start creating an internal story of accomplishment. With each personal milestone achieved, whether big or small, a strong sense of self-assurance is formed. This assurance is propelled by every forward step, which is proof of our mastery over adversities.

It is through empowerment that self-esteem blossoms like a flower given ample nourishment. The chemical rain of dopamine plays a pivotal role in shaping our perceptions of what we are capable of, delivering internal reflections of our past successes and potential future achievements. Alongside this positive feedback loop, a healthy attitude toward one's own abilities and worth primes like a sapling in the sunlight.

Achievement and self-evaluation can be affected by outside sources or distorted viewpoints, like any internal process. An overestimation or harsh criticism of oneself can throw off dopamine levels, affecting one's perception of empowerment. To truly affirm oneself, it is important to maintain equilibrium and a healthy attitude toward both achievement and self-evaluation, allowing dopamine to aid in this pursuit.

Memory

The multifaceted role of dopamine in learning facilitates the consolidation of moments and memories of relevance. The salient moments are enriched with dopamine, embedding them deep in the folds of memory. It is as if dopamine marks each point of wisdom on the neural map, ensuring that they never fade into oblivion.

In its presence, the learning process is infused with a touch of magnetism. The molecule stimulates the circuits of curiosity and attention, transforming the pursuit of knowledge into an interaction of emotions. Each neuron, resonating with the promise of gratification, latches on to the opportunity to acquire novel skills and facts.

Dopamine acts as a sort of internal archive, indexing, and organizing information so that it can be retrieved at the appropriate time. When we dive back into a subject or try to recall an elusive detail, dopamine presents itself as a guide that leads us through memory.

Chapter 3:

Dopamine's Implications on Physical Health

According to the World Health Organization (WHO), neurological disorders are diseases of the central and peripheral nervous systems. In other words, the brain, spinal cord, cranial nerves, peripheral nerves, nerve roots, autonomic nervous system, neuromuscular junction, and muscles. (World Health Organization, 2021)

In brain physiology, dopamine plays a pivotal role in regulating the neuromotor functions. This captivating molecule is fascinatingly so precise that any imbalance in the central nervous system can lead to neurological disorders that translate to physical issues.

Uncontrollable spikes in dopamine lead to dyskinesia, a disorder characterized by involuntary movements that are frequently observed in individuals receiving prolonged treatment for Parkinson's disease with either levodopa or dopamine. These abrupt, unmanageable twitches and contortions vividly highlight how dopamine affects the nerve cells regulating motor function.

Parkinson's disease exhibits apparent symptoms like rigidity, tremors, and problems with the coordination of voluntary movements. But it's the damage done to the brain's structure and chemistry that lies beneath the surface. The black substance's dying dopamine-positive cells highlight this dearth of dopamine production.

Dopamine disruptions can have diverse effects on individuals, ranging from problems with impulse control and concentration, usually linked with ADHD, to anhedonia, which is the inability to experience pleasure.

Along with physical symptoms, these issues can present themselves in a multitude of ways.

Pharmacological research plays a role in providing real solutions for individuals facing ailments related to dopamine levels. To decipher the intricacies of dopamine, modern science adopts a multifaceted methodology using molecular biology, clinical psychology, and neuroimaging to examine the mosaic aspects. These modalities help in re-establishing the equilibrium of the affected individuals.

Scientists probe the connection between brain chemistry and bodily function in the field that is the human body. The interlinking of physical issues with dopaminergic dysregulation proves this complexity. The quest for solutions that are both neurological and physical is fueled by the enigmatic prospect of dopamine. The intriguing relationship between the human body's functions highlights its extraordinary quality.

Metabolic and Hormonal Functions

Dopamine, with its enigmatic power, silently penetrates the complex network of metabolic regulation and intertwines with appetite modulation. This torrid romance with physiology determines body weight and metabolic balance. It promotes satiety, regulating the transition between ingestion and satisfaction, guiding the organism toward the desired balance.

This game of balance, not without nuances, is revealed in the panoramic view of physical health. As we delve deeper into the interaction of dopamine with metabolic mechanisms, a transformative insight emerges. An insight that sheds light on the subtle links between molecular composition and physiological dynamics, manifesting as a complex and fluid canvas where dopamine transcends its role as a mere neuronal transmitter.

The digestive system's connection with dopamine is unquestionably intriguing and enhances our comprehension of human physiology. Despite its well-known effects on the central nervous system, this molecule's impact on the gut is equally impressive, encompassing adjustments to movement, excretion, and nourishment in digestive organs.

Engendering some mystique, dopamine proves to be quite the instructor as it deftly regulates gastrointestinal tissues. Its virtuosic control lies in a balance of inhibition and stimulation. What's more, dopamine's curious penchant for engaging with a range of receptors chemically harmonizes with various reactions, depending on the receptor's own proclivities.

The dual-functional duality of dopamine within the gastrointestinal system must be highlighted as an utmost priority. This neurotransmitter has the power to inhibit intestinal motility at one moment, thus ensuring proper digestion and nutrient absorption, while also instigating muscle contraction and mobilizing intestinal contents at another moment.

Founded upon the distinguished chorus of receptors nestled within the intestinal walls, lies an assorted repertoire of dopamine-crafted reactions. These dopaminergic receptors carry out precise directions from dopamine, dictating what occurs within the gastrointestinal tissues. Each adept and careful selection of either receptor controls whether the motor function will be accelerated or delayed, if the secretory glands will awaken to activity or remain dormant, and if nutrient absorption will be done with haste or prudence.

Under dopamine's sway, the vital hormone regulating lactation and stress response, known as prolactin, is kept in check as well.

To maintain optimal balance, dopamine prohibits the release of prolactin, which is vital in managing lactation-related anxiety. Hormonal equilibrium can be achieved with this hormone effectively regulating systems.

As it turns out, the influence of prolactin is not limited to its effect on lactation or the maternal bond. Rather, this hormone serves a dual purpose by helping to regulate stress and anxiety as well. What's fascinating is that prolactin achieves this by promoting an adaptive response to emotional pressure, thereby expanding its reach beyond just the realm of motherhood.

The pituitary gland's control of the growth hormone's production is most perfected by the brilliance of dopamine. In regulating both growth and metabolism, hormone exchanges rely on dopamine's ability to suppress the hormone via specific receptors.

Of great importance in maintaining thyroid balance is the hormone thyrotropin, which has a unique connection to dopamine, as is common with bodily hormones. One interesting effect of dopamine on thyrotropin is its ability to cause a reverse effect on its release. The release of thyrotropin is promoted by an increase in dopamine, even as growth hormone secretion is inhibited. This exchange highlights dopamine's power to prompt diverse hormonal responses and adjust to different endocrine functions, ensuring the thyroid gland's health.

In the complex hormonal dance that regulates an organism's stress response and homeostasis during challenging situations, dopamine's crucial role cannot be overlooked. Controlling the important hormone corticotropin in the hypothalamic-pituitary-adrenal axis, dopamine functions through a feedback mechanism to negatively regulate the production and release of ACTH. An interplay between dopamine and other hormones adds to the complexity of this system, making it ever-changing.

The endocrine system is a marvel to witness, where the relation between dopamine and prolactin showcases its true complexity. The dynamic story of different forms of prolactin and how dopamine can inhibit it is a fascinating tale of balance within our body. The interconnectedness and interaction of these hormones is truly amazing.

Renal System

Fundamentally regulating fluid balance and blood pressure is the mutual dependence of the adrenal glands and kidneys, with dopamine playing an important role as a key factor. To understand this, one must recognize the interconnectedness between the endocrine and renal systems.

In the midst of strenuous circumstances, constraining blood vessels and escalating blood flow are the proficiencies of adrenaline. These hormones, essential for a surge in blood pressure during "fight-or-flight" scenarios, are stimulated by dopamine, which influences adrenal medulla cells. The adrenal glands have an extraordinary function in maintaining blood pressure and managing stress.

Crucially involved in the different systems processes, dopamine is highly regarded for its ability to regulate. The kidneys, essential organs responsible for fluid and electrolyte balance, are among the many processes under its control. At the fundamental level, it commands the nephrons, the units responsible for filtering and reabsorbing within the kidneys. In order to maintain good health, bodily systems must collaborate effectively, as demonstrated by dopamine's ability to impact both adrenal glands and kidneys. Upon stimulation of dopaminergic receptors, this neurotransmitter can influence the absorption of water and sodium, ultimately leading to effects on blood pressure and water balance. The relationship between dopamine and hormonal regulation in the body is closely linked to kidney function, highlighting its dual purpose in these units.

Disruption in hormonal balance caused by Addison's disease can hinder the adrenal glands' production of adrenaline and noradrenaline, ultimately affecting the body's ability to regulate blood pressure and handle stress. Managing this disorder is an enduring challenge, as malfunctions can persist over extended periods.

Take a journey into the complex correlation between dopamine, kidneys, and adrenal glands and you will discover a riveting story of human physiology. Governing the discharge of adrenaline and noradrenaline from the adrenal glands, dopamine also regulates the levels of reabsorption of water and sodium in the kidneys. This intermingling sets the stage for a labyrinthine connection between blood pressure stability, stress reaction, and electrolyte equilibrium. In essence, the interplay of these components sparks an engrossing physiological adventure.

Movement Control

In the motor system, dopamine acts as the baton that directs refined and coordinated motor responses. Tightly woven into the functional interrelation that connects the challenging movements of thought to the precision of motor execution.

Traversing the winding pathways of the cerebral cortex, dopamine shapes the excitability of motor neurons, refining the impulses that flow from the cortex to the striatum. It lends a multifaceted texture to motor signaling, dictating inhibition or stimulation of motor responses according to context and target.

The numbing potential of dopamine, illustrated by the catastrophic consequences of Parkinson's disease, further illuminates its influence on motor pathways. In this tragic scenario, the degeneration of dopaminergic neurons in the black substance translates into a cruel loss in the coordination of fluid and voluntary movements, plunging those affected into a conflict of disconnection between motor thought and its physical manifestation.

Dopamine deficit, a key piece in the puzzle of motor function, is the protagonist in the emergence of motor symptoms that paint an unmistakable portrait of Parkinson's disease.

A lack of dopamine in neural pathways disrupts the delicate balance between inhibition and excitation, allowing neuronal activity to escape to the confines of coordination. Tremor, manifested in the hands and limbs, manifests the disconnection between mind and body that is characteristic of this condition.

Rigidity, another symptom in this representation, manifests as a relentless embrace of the muscles, an embrace dictated by dopamine deficiency. The resulting muscular rigidity, an involuntary response to unbalanced signaling, becomes an insurmountable obstacle in the quest for fluid, natural movements. Flexibility is distorted into a taut and rigid result, and the patient is faced with the constant struggle against this unwanted yoke.

And, in the penumbra of this motor drama, bradykinesia is like the third piece, emulating an hourglass with its slow temporal flow. The absence of dopamine in the motor pathways slows down nerve impulses, decreasing the speed of response in the execution of movements. Bradykinesia, a decelerated and labored consequence, provides a picture of frustration and effort, where once smooth actions now become a monumental challenge.

On the spectrum of neurological conditions, restless legs syndrome is part of the list. This condition, also known as Willis-Ekbom syndrome, is notable for its manifestation in the lower extremity domain, where incessant sensations prompt the patient to seek relief that often remains elusive.

The neurochemical roots of this sensory juggling can be traced to a disruption in the transmission of nerve signals, particularly in the neurotransmitter dopamine and its influence on motor and sensory pathways. Lack of this substance, or its dysfunction in the motor pathways, causes restlessness that manifests itself in the compulsive need to move the legs, seeking the relief that stillness cannot provide.

Symptoms are characterized by a tingling, burning, itching sensation, or simply a deep restlessness that is aroused when the body reclines to rest. This scenario changes with movement; the act of stretching, moving, or massaging the legs can be a ritual of momentary relief, but often, rest rekindles the irrepressible urge.

Despite its apparent triviality, restless legs syndrome can tinge on the quality of life with dark overtones. Sleep, that restful refuge, is often desecrated by restlessness, leaving the patient with an interrupted wakefulness that affects vitality and general well-being. The resulting fatigue, like a heavy curtain, drapes over the daytime scene, influencing mood and cognitive function.

Physical Activity

Physical endurance, that resilient capacity that allows an organism to extend its sustained activity over time, finds dopamine a distinguished accomplice. Studies have pointed out the influence of this neurotransmitter in the regulation of fatigue, thanks to its role in modulating the subjective perception of effort. By stimulating dopaminergic receptors, the sensation of exhaustion is attenuated, postponing exhaustion and raising the fatigue tolerance threshold. In this perspective, dopamine works as a catalyst that blurs the previously conceived limits of endurance.

Strength, the physical force that lies in the synapse between muscle and nerve, also yields to the influx of dopamine. Studies have fueled the notion that this molecule plays an essential role in facilitating muscle contraction by increasing the firing frequency of motor units. This interaction not only enhances muscle power but also gives muscles a more agile reactivity and more precise execution of movements, providing an optimal setting for the pursuit of physical excellence.

Athletes and regular exercise enthusiasts, in their relentless quest for self-improvement, welcome these revelations with eager eyes. Recognizing the preponderant role of dopamine in endurance and strength, these astute individuals may explore strategies that enhance its production. Regular physical activity, particularly aerobic exercise, has been associated with increases in dopamine release, endorsing an additional incentive to persevere in the sporting routine.

However, excessive manipulation of dopamine levels can trigger challenges, as we have seen, from emotional imbalances to behavioral addictions. A lucid understanding of this neurochemical system prompts a nuanced approach, where the pursuit of performance is juxtaposed with care for mental and physical health.

Cardiovascular Health

In the cardiovascular system, dopamine acts by fine-tuning the heart rate with a sure and precise hand. Through its interaction with dopaminergic receptors located in the heart and arteries, this molecule triggers adjustments that influence the rate and strength of the heartbeat. Dopamine increases the force of cardiac contraction, prompting the heart to beat with a vigorous and coordinated rhythm. In parallel, through other receptors, dopamine directs the dilation of peripheral blood vessels, thereby regulating resistance and blood pressure.

The result reflects the delicate interplay between energy and relaxation, an exchange of hormones and nerve signals that interact in harmony to maintain cardiovascular homeostasis. However, as in any complex plot, nuances are essential. In certain contexts, dopamine can also exert opposing influences on blood pressure regulation, as its action can vary according to dose, location, and situational conditions.

This biochemical balance, however, may falter in the context of health challenges. Conditions such as hypertension or heart failure can throw an unexpected twist into this plot. In the case of heart failure, for example, the receptors' response to dopamine can weaken, contributing to a decrease in the heart's contractile force and exacerbating the failure.

Body Temperature

An area deeply involved in maintaining equilibrium and regulating body temperature is the hypothalamus, situated within the brain. The specific process, also referred to as homeostasis, is achieved through the critical role played by dopamine in directing the various segments of the hypothalamus toward proper thermal regulation.

With its title as the guardian of the gates, the hypothalamus rules over both the nerves and endocrine systems. This dutiful overseer is always on high alert, carefully monitoring the body's temperature. With precision control over temperature regulation, it has the ability to detect even the smallest changes in heat. It's quick to react to fluctuations in the environment, determined to protect the vital inner workings of the body.

Our body temperature fluctuates, but dopamine serves as the leader. Through neural pathways, this chemical thermostat interacts with the hypothalamus, conveying diverse signals to regulate our thermal reactions. Dopamine levels influence our body's temperature to maintain optimal conditions.

Sweat glands create moisture that evaporates to lower body temperature by connecting neurotransmitters to receptors. Triggered by high body temperatures, this process relies on the hypothalamus to regulate blood flow and react to temperature changes. When dopamine signals reach the hypothalamus, it prompts blood vessels to dilate so heat can be released through the skin's surface.

Stepping into the cold, dopamine gets triggered, and the hypothalamus takes action to regulate body temperature. Constricting the blood vessels, heat release is limited to conserve warmth. The body also responds with tight muscle contractions, like a comforting hug, and sweating slows down to retain heat. The changing atmosphere cues this distinct thermoregulatory response from dopamine.

The astounding relation between neurotransmitters and neuroreceptors is what maintains our ideal body temperature. At its core is a conversation between dopamine and the hypothalamus. Our very breath and every beat of our hearts are reflections of the endless exchange of chemicals within us, an intricate and dynamic system essential to our well-being. This is a true testament to the complexity of life.

Chapter 4:

Modern Lifestyle Challenges

Pushing us toward unfamiliar territories, technology is spearheading an enormous shift that we are on the cusp of. We find ourselves amidst constant breakthroughs and a remarkable level of advancement in today's fast-paced, interconnected society. Digitalization and innovation are at the forefront, revolutionizing our typical days.

As the first rays of dawn peek over the horizon, humanity rushes to mobilize. Our reliance on technology is indubitable—it acts as our alarm clock, rousing us with an onslaught of alerts and texts clamoring for our attention. The internet hums with a constant stream of current events, correspondence, and viral phenomena; prompting us to maintain our footing in the rapidly morphing digital realm. Full steam ahead, the passage of time eludes us as we must remain vigilant, or risk being caught in the tumultuous wake of progress.

The work environment has gone through significant shifts as a result of our quick-paced lifestyles. Nowadays, it is tough to differentiate between our personal and work schedules since we are continuously immersed in our jobs. While this adaptation has some advantages, like being more adaptable, it also presents certain difficulties, such as burnout and isolation, that need our attention.

Not everything is negative, limitless possibilities and an enhanced level of convenience have been made available in the world thanks to innovations. It may seem overwhelming, but automation and AI have delivered seamless efficiency and luxurious convenience that deserve recognition. These technological strides have simplified some of the once tedious tasks, freeing up additional time for the pursuit of illustrious and creative desires. In addition, communication gaps have been shortened by globalization, granting us the opportunity to engage with diverse cultures and expand our horizons.

Our modern age places great importance on harmonizing our relationship with technology and the physical world. Taking pleasure in non-screen related experiences, prioritizing personal connections amidst the constant commotion, and finding time for oneself are all factors to consider. Despite the overwhelming presence of digital devices, we are still able to maintain our independence and push back.

We interact with the world amidst a never-ending barrage of information and stimuli originating from numerous sources. This interconnected realm is rife with sensory and cognitive stimulation, drastically reshaping the bases of our environment. The ceaseless stream of data not only shapes our daily experiences but also has a pronounced effect on neural processes that govern dopamine.

Contemporary society is like a flood of information that we are wading through. It can lead to "accustoming"—a weariness that occurs when we are forever bombarded by small and regular incentives. This may affect how we seek gratification and push us to look for more intense or varied input to feel satisfied.

The dopaminergic channels in the brain can be affected by an excess of information, leading to changes in adaptation. The frenzied switching between tasks and the influx of facts hinder the ability to hone concentration and focus. Such a scenario may alter the way in which stimuli are perceived by the brain, affecting dopamine release and response. Another significant factor in this situation is the constant yearning for instantaneous, fresh excitement, which is frequently emphasized in the digital domain. This craving may have an impact on the pattern of dopamine release and possibly limit long-term gratification, while also hindering sustained attention.

Jobs and Routines

While seeking information on this subject, the exploration of sedentary jobs is a topic of inescapable resonance. As societies evolve, the confines of work seem to be leaning toward immobility, and it is here that the relationship with the decline of physical activity requires deep analysis.

In a world where technology flows like an impetuous river for work, we find ourselves surrounded by screens and devices that, despite their apparent convenience, lead us to the threshold of a sedentary lifestyle. The dichotomy between digital frenzy and physical inactivity is drawn in stark inks, and their interaction could be considered a modern dilemma.

Jobs that anchor individuals to ergonomic desks and chairs may underpin work progress, but paradoxically, they can erode physical vitality. The workday has mutated into a reality where hours in front of a screen far exceed minutes of movement. This dissonance between duty and bodily well-being is a phenomenon worthy of examination.

The interconnection between professional life and physical health takes on profound nuances. As sedentary occupations proliferate, physical activity becomes a scarce commodity. The ravages of this investment can impact cardiovascular health, posture, and musculature. However, the equation is not as simple as it sounds. Creativity and problem-solving, inherently present in sedentary work, forge the mind of intellect.

The crossroads at which we find ourselves calls for balanced introspection. Approaches that mitigate the prevalence of sedentary work environments are needed. The design of ergonomic workspaces, the promotion of active breaks, and the assimilation of healthy habits in the work routine emerge as possible concrete solutions.

The study of the exploration of sedentary jobs and their link with the decrease in physical activity unravels a multifaceted narrative. The symbiosis between work performance and bodily well-being requires precise intervention. Although sedentary jobs have taken root in modern society, it is our responsibility to design a routine where dynamism and health cohabit in harmony.

Also, the complexities of the brain and the intricacies of the psyche intersect in the realm of the interplay between dopamine production and human motivation in relation to repetitive and tedious work duties. Investigating the subtleties of this correlation reveals a clear and strong connection.

To experience pleasure and satisfaction, the brain needs a sufficient amount of dopamine. But when it's exposed to monotonous activities, dopamine production can get disrupted, decreasing the chemical's levels and ultimately lowering feelings of gratification. It looks like the brain is craving pleasurable stimuli, but not getting enough of its usual dopamine fix.

When it comes to tackling monotonous tasks on repeat, the intense sensation of gratification and success that flies through us after conquering a stimulating challenge dramatically drops—causing both a lack of inspiration and motivation. The reason for this is a decline in the levels of dopamine, which occurs due to following a routine that is far from stimulating.

The constant nature of repetitive tasks and dopamine production have long-term effects on neural networks and mental agility. Restructuring and forming new connections, also known as brain plasticity, can be hindered by routines lacking unique stimuli. The capacity to adapt could be negatively impacted by limiting opportunities to create neural networks.

Not all downsides of mundane tasks are necessarily negative, as benefits can surface under certain circumstances. For some individuals, repetition can promote heightened efficiency and automation, which can prove fulfilling. It's essential to consider that motivation isn't solely regulated by chemical substances. Factors such as one's work environment, sense of purpose, and connections with peers can play a substantial role in how well one manages recurrent obligations. Nevertheless, positions that showcase the most conspicuous indicators of monotony and repetition seem to lack these attributes.

Digital Devices

Our era is characterized by the habitual presence of various technological devices that are ubiquitous in our everyday lives. This intimacy with gadgets has given us novel means of seeking entertainment, acquiring knowledge, and staying connected. The mere anticipation of a notification or message can trigger a surge of dopamine and pleasure.

This anticipatory attitude is innate in our biological reward system, always striving for immediate satisfaction.

Social networks, meanwhile, have emerged as platforms that encourage virtual social interaction and exposure to varied stimuli. The dynamics of "likes," comments, and shares on these platforms generate a kind of feedback loop where each positive interaction triggers a dopamine release response. This social validation process, often instantaneous and quantifiable in the form of virtual numbers and reactions, can become a powerful online pleasure-seeking engine.

Apps, especially those designed with a gamification strategy, skillfully capitalize on dopamine release to keep users engaged and motivated. Unlocking levels, accumulating points, and virtual rewards generate an addictive cycle where each achievement is accompanied by short but intense momentary satisfaction. This deliberate design, backed by knowledge of how the human brain works, is a testament to how technology can harness our basic neurological responses to keep us immersed in its platforms.

However, it is of an urgent nature to recognize that this constant interaction with digital devices and online activities can have multifaceted effects on our mental health and well-being. While dopamine release can provide rewarding stimulation, over-reliance on these stimuli can lead to an endless search for validation, negatively affecting self-esteem and perception of reality. Overexposure to digital stimuli can also lead to concentration problems and disconnection from real-world experiences.

The term "dopaminergic loop" refers to this feedback loop in the brain we mentioned that involves the release of dopamine. This cycle of reward and gratification can lead to addictive behaviors. As we constantly seek that instant gratification that comes from technology, we can fall into a pattern where our attention is caught in a continuous search for digital stimuli. The urge to repeatedly check our social networks, emails, and mobile apps becomes an ingrained behavior, similar to how a person might crave an addictive substance.

The complexity of the problem lies in how technology is designed to keep us engaged. Personalized recommendation algorithms are based on collecting data about our preferences and habits, allowing platforms to present us with content that they know will appeal to us. This insightful and highly personalized approach further increases the release of dopamine, thus fueling the addictive cycle.

The dynamics of technology addiction can vary in intensity and in the impact it has on each individual's daily life. Some people may find it difficult to focus on important tasks due to the constant digital temptation, while others may feel a decrease in their face-to-face personal relationships due to a preference for online interaction. It is critical to recognize that technology in itself is not inherently harmful, but its uncontrolled use can lead to significant problems.

Mindful use of technology requires setting boundaries on our digital interaction and promoting activities that facilitate human connection. It's vital to cultivate awareness and self-regulation to combat technology addiction. By creating technology-free areas, we can further this goal.

Chronic Stress From Work

Professional situations that are excessive and inflexible can often become too much to bear, resulting in chronic stress that exceeds an individual's ability to cope. Workplace stress factors may include clashing environments or the presence of long-term stressors alongside rigid deadlines and constant workloads. The body reacts with physiological responses over time due to the prolonged stress, activating the hypothalamic-pituitary-adrenal (HPA) axis. Consequently, cortisol is released from this hormonal pathway, which has been associated with the stress response.

Amid ongoing stress, the neurotransmitter dopamine undergoes changes in both release and response to receptors. This disrupts dopamine levels and causes a disruption in pleasure and reward. The eventual decrease in motivation leads to exhaustion and burnout.

Altered dopamine production and processing receptors in the brain may happen due to prolonged exposure to stress, which is being studied for its link to chronic stress. Such a phenomenon could lead to a malfunction of the reward system and make it hard for one to find joy in their work or other enjoyable things. The genes responsible for dopamine production are thought to be affected by stress, thus contributing to this outcome.

Disrupted Sleep Patterns

Nowadays, poor sleep quality is often linked to the integration of digital connectivity and artificial lighting. People frequently use smartphones, tablets, and computers, exposing themselves to blue light emissions that suppress melatonin production. As a result, sleep onset difficulties and insomnia may arise, significantly impacting time management. It has been found that prolonged exposure to these emissions has a direct impact on regulating one's sleep cycle.

Excessive dopamine release resulting from indulging in online activities can overstimulate the brain's reward circuits and cause poor dopamine regulation. Furthermore, exposing oneself to screens for extended periods during the night can worsen the issue, leading to decreased dopamine responsiveness.

Taking several measures can alleviate the detrimental effects of modern routines on sleep and dopamine levels. A crucial step is abstaining from using digital devices for at least an hour before sleep to diminish melatonin disturbance. Furthermore, cultivating sleep hygiene habits, such as crafting a tranquil, dim bedroom atmosphere, is pivotal to ensuring excellent quality sleep.

Eating Habits

Undergoing significant changes are our eating habits during this social transformation era. The regulation of neurotransmitters, such as dopamine, is pivotal in these transformations and has an impact not only on our physical well-being but also alters our brain biochemistry.

When we indulge in modern diets, we often find satisfaction in the short term due to the presence of refined sugars and saturated fats. However, what is surprising is the undeniable connection that exists between our dopamine levels and eating habits.

The undeniable proof of the harm that ultra-processed foods can cause to one's well-being and dopamine production within the brain is growing. Such products are frequently linked to a craving for immediate satisfaction, which merely compounds the problem. An overabundance of dopamine stimulation is the root of the concern, resulting in a reduction of sensitivity. This is ultimately responsible for a diminished receptiveness to the very substance that plays the role. From being unable to enjoy anything else besides food, the consequences of this unhappiness impact the brain's reward circuit related to food consumption. A long-term issue that definitely commands our full and unwavering concentration.

Habits of modern eating are interfering with the link between dopamine and motivation. In a world where high-calorie food is readily available, gratification is experienced immediately, leading to a decline in perseverance and determination toward long-term objectives. With dopamine playing a role in visualizing and concentrating on future endeavors, this vicious cycle indirectly affects levels of dopamine.

To manage the harmful influences of current eating routines on dopamine production, it's essential to adopt a measured and sensible consumption approach. An ideal consumption routine should involve the inclusion of various nutrient-rich foods, which include veggies, lean proteins, healthy fats, and fruits, to maintain optimal brain function and healthy dopamine levels. Conversely, the potential to satisfy oneself with non-food achievements is necessary to establish a healthy tie between motivation and dopamine.

Interpersonal Relationships

Our dopamine levels have grown increasingly linked to alterations in how we interact and bond with one another, thanks to novel methods of human connections. These unique modes have brought about a series of impactful shifts we are yet to fully comprehend.

An environment in which instant gratification has become a norm due to the modern human interactions that are marked by the presence of virtual interactions and online dating platforms is more prevalent with time. A small dose of happiness, comparable to a neurochemical response, is produced, which reinforces the need to further participate in these virtual interactions, providing gratification.

The relationship between dopamine levels and innovative forms of human interaction can't be ignored. It's worth noting the downside, which is a potential decrease in satisfaction from in-person interactions and a higher likelihood of anxiety and depression when digital expectations aren't met.

The convenience of constant digital communication is not enough for genuine and meaningful connections- it simply lacks the emotional depth that occurs in physical interactions. Brevity and fragmentation further hinder the establishment of such connections, leading to a sense of isolation and loneliness. These negative emotions essentially nullify the positive effects of dopamine.

As online communication methods become more popular, there is a looming risk of us relying too heavily on the internet for communication. Unfortunately, this shift may put our social and emotional skills in real life in peril. With the convenience and quickness of digital communication, we may start to avoid in-person conversations that could be uncomfortable. Essentially, the ease of online communication could hinder our ability to handle complex relationships face-to-face. Overcompensation on virtual communication can deteriorate our nonverbal understanding, including interpreting emotions through faces and body posture, as well as empathy for others, causing a decrease over time. To prevent this from happening, we must recognize the potential danger and strive for an equilibrium where digital and physical relationships complement each other. This way, we will protect our intrinsic capability to form authentic and valuable human relationships.

Cultivating genuine human connections can be challenging in today's virtual age. Emotional dependency, lack of tangible connection, and unhealthy coping mechanisms can arise. Therefore, striking a balance between virtual interactions and in-person interactions is crucial. Doing so ensures that we mitigate these negative consequences and instead foster more valuable and fulfilling relationships.

Chapter 5:

Dopamine Detox and Its Benefits

Over time, you may find yourself needing sweeter foods to achieve the same satisfaction as that first heavenly bite of a delicious pastry. However, to regain better habits and control the negative factors that affect our health, dopamine detoxification is an option to consider. The process entails curbing the addictive effects of dopamine on the brain to improve our well-being. With regards to dopamine, experiencing highly rewarding stimuli in excess can cause a similar "tolerance" where additional dopamine is required to reach the same level of pleasure. It is important to note that this outcome can arise from any of the techniques mentioned earlier that create noteworthy or trivial alterations in dopamine levels.

The mental health repercussions of constant overstimulation are concerning. Natural rewards like daily activities or reaching goals can become less enjoyable due to desensitized dopamine receptors. Too much dopamine exposure can also create addictions and lasting emotional instability. Oddly-named brain chemicals can majorly affect one's well-being.

Electronics and food, among other things, can trigger the release of dopamine, and overexposure can desensitize our receptors. A strategy to reverse this phenomenon is to take a break, or detox from dopamine triggers. This activity-restoration technique can restore balance and promote better brain health, similar to how abstaining from pastries can rekindle taste sensitivity. Part of the approach is to limit engagement in dopamine-releasing activities, such as overusing devices or consuming ultra-processed foods.

Artificial rewards can create a dependence that dulls dopamine receptors. To get them firing again, exposure to stimuli needs to be reduced. Once natural sensitivity returns, the enjoyment of small pleasures can be restored. Detoxing dopamine also expands curiosity and creates a more holistic life full of new experiences and hobbies.

Also, improved attention span and reduced mental fatigue can be achieved by restoring dopamine-related neural pathways. This is because efficient neural communication helps transmit information in the brain, leading to better mental acuity, focus, and cognitive clarity. In turn, this can have a beneficial effect on overall mental health.

Achieving greater emotional stability involves minimizing the constant thirst for immediate gratification to improve mood swings. A brain that is not distressed about receiving rewards eliminates the possibility of unexpected mood swings and allows for deeper emotional understanding. This opens up opportunities for introspection and emotional bonding.

When one undergoes the dopamine detox, they may find that it surprisingly increases productivity. By eliminating constant stimuli, the brain can better concentrate on essential tasks, which ultimately enhances the ability to maintain focus for extended periods. The end result is a heightened work productivity and an overall sense of contentment.

Promoting brain health and well-being in today's world full of rewarding stimuli requires a dopamine detox. This detox allows dopamine receptors to recover their natural sensitivity, restoring balance and increasing satisfaction in daily tasks. Giving the brain a break from heightened dopaminergic stimulation is like letting a garden lie to prosper.

How to Do a Dopamine Detox

Amidst the inundation of stimulants, the notion of digital detox is a welcomed relief. Essentially, it is a conscious and purposeful practice of severing ties with the electronic gadgets and virtual platforms that have taken over our focus so completely.

In our modern world, we're inundated with constant connection. But in order to reclaim our own agency over our thoughts and time, it's essential to unplug and find balance. This disconnection doesn't just entail shutting off our devices or silencing notifications, but rather, it's an internal journey toward inner peace and mindfulness. With so many distractions vying for our attention, it's become imperative to take a moment to reflect and simply be present in the now.

Embracing a digital detox involves a broad range of measures that can be subtle or extensive. Initially, adopting simple habits like reducing our social media activity, muting disruptive pop-up messages, and scheduling fixed periods to check our inbox can enhance our mental agility and emotional health. Such modifications can boost our performance and improve our engagement with the environment and humanity.

Entering the field of external stimulus reduction is a crucial aspect of digital detox since it encourages the filtering of the information we absorb. The aim of external stimulus reduction is to counteract the overwhelming amount of data and selectively decide what deserves our focus. Thus, we can exercise more control over the information we consume by making informed decisions about what merits our attention.

Fostering a genuine interaction space and facilitating introspection and creativity requires being selective about the sources of external stimuli. Quality needs to be weighed against quantity when cultivating an information diet that is enriching instead of overwhelming. This helps preserve one's mental health while also promoting authenticity.

Finding balance in a digital world takes intentional effort through acts like reducing external stimuli and detoxification. By doing so, we can better control our time and attention, which grants us meaningful reconnection with ourselves and the world around us.

Full or Gradual Detox

Let's start by examining a radical strategy: total detoxification. This entails an abrupt abandonment of the pleasurable substance or behavior responsible for your addiction. The logic behind this method is to smother your brain's hyperactive dopamine receptors by removing all sources of stimulation. Although this approach can be useful in extreme cases of addiction requiring a dramatic overhaul, it also poses significant risks. Abruptly stopping dopamine production can lead to severe withdrawal symptoms, making the experience arduous and miserable.

In less severe dependence, individuals often turn to gradual tapering, which progressively reduces consumption of the addictive substance. This method facilitates a smoother and more controlled transition to balanced dopamine levels. It's beneficial in decreasing the intensity of withdrawal symptoms and in allowing bodies and brains to adjust comfortably to changes. On the flip side, immediate cessation of substance consumption is the opposite of gradual tapering.

The various approaches to addiction breakage each have their own pros and cons to contemplate. Abruptly ending addictive behaviors with full detoxification can be successful yet overwhelming, given the strength of withdrawal symptoms. Conversely, easing off gradually might be more pleasant for the patient, but it may involve extended periods and necessitate enhanced self-control. The preference between the two approaches hinges on the individual experience, the intensity of dependency, and personal predilections.

Addressing dependency on substances that affect brain dopamine levels can be achieved through two unique approaches: gradual reduction or total detoxification, each with its own advantages and challenges. The preferred method should be determined based on individual needs and circumstances. It's important to note that seeking professional assistance can ensure a safe and effective process toward recovery. So, whether you opt for a gradual dwindling-off or a complete detox, remember that help is available.

A Detox Plan

The path to healing will become clear with a companion providing step-by-step guidance. Articulating the complex nuances of your progress using written language alone is an insurmountable task.

Self-Assessment and Awareness

In the first step, establishing a solid groundwork for change requires reflection and evaluation of your dopamine-releasing activities. Patterns and triggers associated with social media, video games, and junk food necessitate consideration. It's essential to scrutinize these specific activities before proceeding.

Clear Goal Setting

Once you have a thorough understanding of your situation, define concrete and achievable goals. These goals should be designed to gradually reduce exposure to dopamine stimuli, without feeling overwhelmed. Setting specific goals helps maintain focus and direction.

Creating an Action Plan

Devising a detailed plan is essential to succeed in your dopamine detox. This could include alternative, healthy activities that gradually increase your satisfaction without relying on artificial stimuli. Explore options such as regular exercise, reading, meditation, and socializing.

Smart Boundaries and Restraints

To maintain a proper balance, set limits and restrictions on access to dopamine sources. For example, you can schedule specific times to check social media or play video games, rather than constantly and uncontrollably. These limits promote self-regulation and prevent overindulgence.

Progressive Integration of Changes

Instead of a radical approach, consider adopting changes gradually. This allows your mind and body to adapt more effectively to new patterns. Over time, your dopamine receptors may adjust, decreasing the need for excessive stimulation.

Social Support and Accountability

Social support and accountability are important for creating a nurturing environment. Given a sense of responsibility to others, people are more inclined to take steps toward accomplishing their ambitions. Being bolstered by friends, family, or communities with comparable objectives can mentally fire up and disburden those who might feel isolated. Advancing toward common goals provides a sense of collective effort, which builds a positive and stimulating atmosphere.

Self-Care Patterns

Sustain inspiration and conquer impulses by prioritizing self-care throughout your journey. Managing stress, eating a nutritious diet, and getting enough rest are all essential in sustaining the optimal functioning of your neurotransmitters, especially dopamine. Remember to never underestimate the significance of self-care.

Ongoing Assessment and Adjustment

Creating a dopamine detox plan is an ongoing and evolving process. Regularly evaluate your progress and adjust your goals as needed. Celebrating achievements is also important to maintaining motivation and a sense of accomplishment.

Extra Tips for Success

Withdrawal symptoms and cravings in dopamine detoxification can vary in intensity and duration depending on individual factors and the extent of previous exposure to dopaminergic stimuli.

Modifying your environment to minimize craving triggers can be highly effective. Eliminating or reducing exposure to stimuli that trigger dopamine release, such as excessive social networking or online gambling, can decrease the intensity of cravings.

Setting healthy goals and rewards can help replace the gratification you used to get from dopaminergic behaviors. Achieving these goals can trigger the release of dopamine in a natural and positive way.

Our hobbies and leisure pursuits shouldn't be underestimated in their ability to influence us. Taking an interest in something we truly love, be it playing an instrument, painting, or solving complex puzzles, can trigger brain pathways that cause dopamine to surge. Plus, as we work to improve our skills in our chosen pastime, we encounter moments of contentment and triumph that are closely tied to the release of this pleasure-inducing neurotransmitter.

Our mental health is certainly boosted by socialization. We cannot discount the value of human interactions in releasing dopamine, be it a good time spent with buddies or a deep conversation with someone special. Our brain produces this chemical as a way of incentivizing us to keep seeking interpersonal relationships. Thanks to technology, we can now even get our dose of dopamine from video chats and browsing social media platforms.

During this time, effectively managing stress demands a well-strategized approach. It is important to implement reliable stress-handling techniques to ensure a smoother transition.

"Mindfulness" is a viable strategy in the given situation. The practice, also known as mindfulness meditation, requires accepting the present moment without judging one's feelings or thoughts. Commencing this meditation routine can enhance cognitive ability and facilitate focusing on the present. This increased awareness could deter the release of excess dopamine, which could potentially provoke nervous actions.

Tame your thoughts by embracing small moments throughout the day to concentrate on the flow of air in your lungs and letting your mind drift. By practicing the art of being mindful of your breathing, you can redirect your thoughts and achieve greater peace of mind. You'll experience a remarkable decrease in stress levels as you fully commit to this beneficial exercise.

For a tranquil experience that eliminates stress, keep a keen watch over your body's sensations for tightness or discomfort. Pause briefly and allow yourself time to recognize any physical feelings and ponder upon them. Take a moment to reflect on your emotional and physical reactions.

Taking care to show kindness to oneself during the process of detoxifying from dopamine is something to take seriously, given the emotional ups and downs that typically come with it. Self-compassion plays a central role in this procedure, as it can be a game-changing approach. Treating oneself with the same level of empathy and compassion as one would extend to a close confidant following a misstep is a helpful approach.

Imbuing your routine with simple joys, such as luxuriating with a warm cup of tea, relishing in calming melodies, and basking amidst nature's wonders, can markedly elevate your tranquility and well-being. Incorporating these unhurried pastimes into your day-to-day life can exert a profound impact on your emotional composure and bliss.

Practicing mindfulness during detoxification yields an array of benefits that extend beyond measures and cultivate a deep connection between oneself and the world, leading to profound well-being. This powerful connection comes from improved emotional regulation and self-awareness, which leads to long-lasting psychological benefits. It's imperative to understand that utilizing mindfulness as a tool can improve all aspects of one's life.

Building Healthy Habits

Being completely detached from technology in this day and age is improbable, which is why people have resorted to conscious consumption of electronic devices. This method is great for reconnecting with technology after a detox period. Conscious consumption involves being mindful and careful in our communication with digital media and stimuli, to facilitate a harmonious proportion between our online and offline lives, and encourage a more profound feeling of mental health.

Here's a hypothetical situation: You open up your device and find yourself bombarded with a flood of notifications, messages, emails, and online material. Your first thought may be to immediately browse through everything, but this is where being conscious about what you consume comes into play. Instead of giving in to the impulse, you pause to ponder what is truly relevant and beneficial at present. To achieve this, a blend of being aware of yourself and being disciplined is necessary.

Choosing to actively control your digital experience can be referred to as "informed choice" or "digital mindfulness," among other terms. Essentially, the goal is to prioritize a deeper, more meaningful immersion in online content over superficial browsing. By doing so, we take ownership of our digital experiences.

Keeping your focus on your goals is key. Before you mindlessly open any websites or apps, take a moment to set clear intentions. Ask yourself whether you're searching for certain information or simply passing time. Such an approach can help you sidestep aimless drifting.

To keep your mind from wandering, limit online activities and disable irrelevant notifications. Establishing a strict timeline will reduce disturbances and enable you to concentrate on pressing assignments.

Enriching your knowledge and perspectives can be achieved by opting for reliable and meaningful sources of information, which is fundamentally content curation. Rather than falling for the "easy click," consuming quality content is essential in this process.

Your well-being can be improved by unplugging from electronic devices and achieving digital rest. Schedule specific times for this purpose to give your mind a break.

Reflect periodically on your online habits with a self-evaluation. Check if you're being inundated with information or if you're allocating too much time to the digital world. Alter your behavior accordingly.

Enriching your online and offline life by practicing conscious consumption of digital media and stimuli means taking charge of your online experience. It's a process of evolving, being aware, making informed choices, and tuning in while living in a world filled with distractions. Navigating digital oceans with clarity and purpose will help you attain your goal.

Benefits and Outcomes

Exposed to constant dopamine-releasing stimuli, maintaining focus on tasks that demand cognitive effort can become very challenging. Nevertheless, this problem is solved by performing a dopamine detox, which is known for its ability to improve one's concentration and focus. Immediate reduction of dopaminergic overstimulation provides a better ability to concentrate on work, studies, or any activity that requires attention.

Exposure to electronic devices and other stimuli that increase dopamine levels can disrupt sleeping patterns, which makes dopamine detoxification beneficial for improved sleep quality. The reduction of dopaminergic stimulation before bedtime can provide relaxation and more restful slumbers. Say goodbye to negative effects on your sleep by limiting your dopamine levels!

Anxiety can be mitigated through dopamine detoxification. Prolonged dopaminergic stimulation can cause anxiety by constantly alerting the brain. Avoiding activities that produce dopamine can decrease anxiety levels, providing a newfound inner peace and tranquility.

Concentration, sleep, and anxiety levels can be rapidly improved through dopamine detox, although it should be noted that everyone's response will be unique. A gradual change may be observed by some, while others experience a quicker shift. To ensure the avoidance of feeling deprived and frustrated, a balanced and sustainable detoxification approach is important to maintain.

Chapter 6:

Exercises for Positive Stimulation

Our body transforms into an experimental laboratory of chemical reactions during intense activity such as weightlifting or running. Inside us, dopaminergic neurons start working to discharge dopamine in precise amounts, as we perspire and push ourselves.

The sensation of reward is released when we put in more effort, creating a bidirectional relationship between effort and reward. We feel motivated to reach the next level of effort by enjoying this sensation. Dopamine release grows as we increase our physical effort. Our brain recognizes and cheers our athletic achievements with a chemical explosion of internal applause. The euphoria and satisfaction we often feel after a strenuous workout are due to this reason.

Evidence suggests that dopamine can impact our eagerness to exercise, adding to the feedback loop between dopamine and exercise. Those with elevated dopamine levels display a larger urge for physical activity, strengthening the notion that exercise and dopamine have a two-way connection. Meanwhile, exercise prompts the discharge of dopamine.

Glimpsed in this intricate chemical scenario is the significance of physical exercise in propelling not only physical wellness but also mental wellness. Our natural inclination to remain active is compounded with intrigue by dopamine, which acts as a mediator of motivation and reward. The enigma surrounding the connection between our bodies and minds is continuously unfolding, and dopamine holds a key role in this. It reminds us that every move we make, every stretch we do, and every bead of perspiration that drips enriches our existence. It is these small accomplishments that make each day exceptional.

Positive Effects

A plethora of positive outcomes stem from the release of dopamine. The initial and foremost result was the pleasure experienced during the aforementioned exercise. This feeling of accomplishment has a significant impact on the impetus to persist in physical exertion. This leads to a cycle of success where the dopamine release improves the disposition and aids the likelihood of adhering to a consistent workout regimen.

At the end of physical activity, the benefits we reap from dopamine do not dissipate. Our post-workout phase is largely influenced by this chemical. After the intense routine of exercises, dopamine is immediately working on the sense of accomplishment and well-being. People often refer to this sensation as the "high," and it is not an overstatement, this is biologically generated as an outcome after physical activity flooding dopamine in our system. In this scenario, dopamine serves as a validation of the contribution we decide to make to our mental and physical health. It works as a star sticker on our forehead after doing something good for ourselves.

During and after exercise, dopamine release and satisfaction exhibit a complex relationship that is not merely chemical. Various influential facets, such as genetics and dopamine receptor sensitivity, impact the intensity of this reaction. Moreover, when dopamine interacts with other neurotransmitters like serotonin, it adds an extra level of fascination to this neurochemical account.

And it does not stop there, boosting our mood and battling stress, anxiety, and depression can be achieved by exercising. The reason behind this is that endorphins are also released when doing physical activity, and they work as natural pain relievers. This enhances dopamine's job of helping our brain counteract the negative effects of stress and anxiety through this powerful interaction. Many researchers have studied the benefits of mental health and physical activity success.

The feeling of getting rid of stress and diverting attention away from your routine concerns is amazing, it can be accomplished by exercise through these chemical reactions. Through physical movements, you let out bottled-up energy, giving it a way out to escape. An engaging break like this acts as therapy for your mind against all emotional turbulence, providing an opportunity to embrace the present.

For a comprehensive plan, it's crucial to keep in mind that addressing stress, anxiety, and depression requires more than exercise alone. Although it can be beneficial for some individuals, other methods should also be employed. A holistic method is suggested to achieve optimal results.

On Brain Health

Exploring the effects of exercise on brain health reveals a web of intertwined positive impacts. It's not just about strengthening the body—regular exercise offers remarkable benefits for the brain as well.

Brain health can greatly benefit from regular exercise, as it triggers a variety of positive effects. Of these benefits, the brain's preservation is most commendable due to its neuroprotective effects. This effect arises from the increase in blood flow and oxygenation throughout the brain, which fosters the development of brain cells.

Exercise promotes the production of molecules in charge of neural growth factors, and it also amplifies the creation of new neural connections. Brain plasticity, as we can recall, is the ability to adapt and learn, this action is bolstered by these substances as well. Furthermore, the molecules mentioned are integral factors in the survival, development, and communication between neurons.

Improvements in cognitive function, memory, and information processing can be derived from stronger neural pathways, akin to information highways in the brain. Regular exercise is an effective method of reinforcing these pathways, leading to better signal transmission between various brain regions. This ultimately results in greater synchronization and cognitive sharpness.

Neurogenesis, the formation of new brain cells, can be kickstarted through exercise, which can, in turn, provide the brain with a protective coat. This coat minimizes the likelihood of age-determined cognitive decline as well as reduces the chances of neurological disorders occurring. As a result, exercise becomes an excellent instrument for preserving brain health over time.

With no uncertainty, the effect of routine physical activity on brain wellness is unshakable. The advantages go beyond the physical to cellular and neural bonding. When we comprehend the affirmative outcome of exercise on the brain, we can make rational choices and improve both our body and psyche.

With all its phases, neural function reaps abundant benefits from multiple brain activities that bolster mental agility. Optimizing our mental faculties encompasses a surprising contribution by physical exercise. A fascinating disclosure is uncovered as we probe deeper into the connection linking cognitive function and physical activity.

Internal archives of experience and knowledge are stored in memory, which can be enhanced through physical activity. Hormones, including brain-derived neurotrophic factors, are released during exercise and act as a fertilizer for brain cells, allowing them to better retain information. This process fortifies short-term memory and alters long-term memory for more effective learning and application.

Regular exercise can enhance attention, improving the internal compass that guides our concentration. Mental clarity and focus are promoted when the hippocampus is stimulated during exercise. However, the release of endorphins and serotonin—known for reducing stress and anxiety, as we mentioned—can also distract and disperse attention.

Each movement becomes an act of brain empowerment in the journey toward cognitive enhancement through exercise, revealing an exquisite interaction between physical energy and mental acuity. For sculpting our cognitive power, exercise presents diverse options that range from walking to running, yoga to weight lifting.

Finding the Right Amount of Exercise

The "Goldilocks zone," a term that evokes the children's story of the three bears, encapsulates a fascinating concept in various fields, especially neuroscience and psychology. This metaphor extends to the search for optimal balance, just as the protagonist was searching for the perfectly tempered soup.

In neuroscience, the "Goldilocks zone" applies to the delicate balance between stimulation and overstimulation of the brain. When we immerse ourselves in challenging but achievable tasks, neural circuits are activated that promote the release of dopamine. It is as if our brain is attracted to the "golden meaning" of challenge and achievement.

Amidst this tale, the champion is dopamine output, on the hunt for the just-right broth tempestuously. When presented with a task that is elementary, levels of dopamine dwindle, as the mind can't seem to locate the necessary spark. Conversely, when the feat is insurmountable, dopamine might vanish, and instead of finding contentment, we encounter vexation.

This phenomenon is reflected in everyday life. Imagine someone who writes. If the task is too easy, such as copying an already known text, dopamine will hardly be activated. But if the task is intriguing but not too complex, such as exploring a new topic, dopamine will flow as he or she faces the challenge and experiences the satisfaction of learning something new.

The "Goldilocks zone" illustrates how finding the sweet spot between boredom and overwhelm can catalyze dopamine production. Thus, when we pursue tasks that fall in this sweet spot of challenge, stimulation, and accomplishment, we are prone to experience a sense of gratification and renewed motivation.

In the context of exercise, the key is finding the perfect balance. If you don't keep active, you may not trigger enough dopamine to feel satisfied, leading to a sense of apathy. However, overexerting yourself can overload your brain's pleasure circuits and leave you feeling desensitized to joy.

The optimal dose of exercise varies from person to person, as our brain's response to physical activity is influenced by genetics, fitness level, and neural sensitivity. To achieve a balance, we must acknowledge the individuality of the response.

Going at an exercise routine with prudence entails finding a middling balance between being overburdened and not being active enough. To get a harmonious dopaminergic reaction, change your activities throughout the week with options like jogging or taking a dip. When you're too strict, you tend to overexert yourself, which goes counter to the original goal. As we move forward, testing what works for us and tweaking it, could help us to be more receptive.

Habit Establishment

This rewarding sensation becomes an internal motivator to repeat the behavior, which in turn contributes to healthy habit formation. This creates a positive feedback loop: the more we exercise, the stronger the connection between physical activity and the pleasurable sensation generated by dopamine becomes.

Motivation and drive are boosted once the habit is formed, and consistent exercise plays a role here. Basically, exercising consistently enhances not just the habit, but also the motivation to stay committed.

Among individuals, habit formation is not a simple, straight progression, due to important factors such as genetics, environment, and personality. These factors shape our reactions to dopamine release and contribute to developing permanent habits. Another critical element impacting the speed of habit formation is the range of physical exercises; their intensity and regularity may alter dopamine release, hence influencing how fast a habit forms.

Overcoming Barriers

Maintaining a consistent exercise routine can be tough due to the various obstacles we encounter. These hurdles can vary from not having enough time to not feeling motivated enough. Nevertheless, overcoming these difficulties and developing a long-lasting workout regimen can be achieved with the right tactics.

In the new era where work has become the main priority, finding the time to exercise and dedicate an hour to ourselves seems uncommon, this translates into hurdles to fit the physical activities to our routines. However, we can trick this hurdle if we are creative and opt for brief spurts of physical activity rather than long periods. We could do things like choosing the stairs instead of the elevator and short stretching sessions during work breaks.

Commitment to exercise can be hindered by a lack of motivation, but we can overcome this by discovering enjoyable physical activities such as dancing, swimming, or team sports. Motivation can also be nurtured by setting achievable goals and rewarding ourselves for progress.

Participating in a sedentary lifestyle can be a byproduct of being too comfortable. To combat this predicament, we can infuse minuscule modifications into our everyday habits, choosing to walk or bike instead of driving for short distances. Making these efforts ensures regular physical activity.

Excessive self-criticism and the fear of failure are significant hurdles that need to be surmounted. However, adopting a kinder approach can be a productive way to overcome these struggles. Acknowledge that each minor breakthrough is valuable, and disappointments are unavoidable. If we internalize this mindset, we can ease the burden placed on ourselves by ourselves, and progress with more confidence.

To maintain steady levels of dopamine, the chemical behind euphoria, we must explore diverse exercise methods. Brain function thrives on originality; therefore, switching up routines can enhance fascination and bliss.

Routine for Exercises at Home

This routine focuses on basic exercises that require no special equipment and can be done in your home space. Remember to warm up before and stretch after.

To warm up, do gentle jumping jacks for three minutes, arm and leg swings, and similar movements to gradually raise your heart rate and prepare your muscles for another five minutes.

The duration of the full-body exercises should be modified according to your preference and adaptation. Perform each exercise for 45 seconds, followed by 15 seconds of rest. These exercises are designed to repeat the cycle three times.

Squats

Begin in a standing position, feet hip-width apart and back straight. Keep your eyes straight ahead and shoulders relaxed. Extend arms forward or place hands on hips for balance.

Begin the movement by bending your knees and hips at the same time, as if you were sitting in an imaginary chair. Be sure to keep your heels on the floor at all times and avoid bringing your knees forward past your toes.

Lower until your thighs are approximately parallel to the floor, keeping your back straight and chest lifted. Keep your knees in line with your feet and keep them from sliding inward or outward.

To return to the starting position, push through the heels, extending the knees and hips at the same time. Keep your core active throughout the movement to provide stability to your back. Remember to inhale on the way down and exhale on the way up.

Knee Bends

Knee push-ups, also known as "half squats" or "partial squats," are an effective exercise for working your leg muscles and glutes.

Start in a standing position, with your feet hip-width apart and your back straight. You can place your hands on your hips or extend your arms forward for balance.

Bend your knees and hips at the same time, as if you were sitting in an imaginary chair. Unlike full squats, here you won't go too low. The idea is to descend only to a comfortable, manageable depth.

Keep your heels on the floor and keep your knees from sliding forward past your toes. Keep your back straight and chest elevated throughout the movement.

Once you reach the desired depth, return to the starting position by pushing through the heels and extending the knees and hips at the same time.

Plank

The plank exercise is a highly effective way to strengthen the core and improve upper body stability.

Start in a plank position, resting your forearms and toes on the floor. Make sure your elbows are in line with your shoulders and your forearms are parallel to each other.

Maintain a straight line from your head to your heels, keeping your hips from sinking or rising. Activate the abdominal and gluteal muscles to keep the position stable.

Look down, keeping the neck in alignment with the spine. Do not let the head hang or the back arch.

Hold this position for as long as you can maintain good form. Start with short intervals, such as 20-30 seconds, and gradually increase as you feel stronger.

To finish, gently lower your knees to the floor and rest. It's better to maintain proper form for a shorter time than to compromise technique by holding the position longer.

After the cycle, you should perform gentle stretches to relax the muscles and reduce the heart rate gradually for about seven minutes.

Aerobic Ideas at Home

There are several options to perform cardiovascular or aerobic exercises comfortably at home. You can jump rope, a simple but effective activity that only requires a rope and enough space. Burpees combine jumping jacks, push-ups, and squats in a single movement, intensifying the heart rate. Marching or running in place is a basic but effective way to get your heart rate up, and you can customize the intensity by lifting your knees higher or varying the pace. If you're looking for fun, dancing in your living room is an excellent option, providing both cardiovascular exercise and a boost in mood.

Using the stairs in your home is also effective for cardio, as is performing boxing exercises in the air, such as jabs and hooks. If you have an exercise bike or elliptical at home, these are excellent options for a more traditional cardio workout.

The challenge lies in devising a plan that balances the energetic cadence of the day-to-day with the quest for constant progress. Each individual is tasked with decoding his or her own physical and mental code, deciphering the signals the body emits, and translating them into strategically selected movements.

From the purposeful steps of cardiovascular training to the leisurely poses of yoga, the repertoire is vast and eclectic. Each routine should be imbued with variability and challenge, avoiding stagnation and encouraging sustained growth. Each individual needs a personalized approach to reach his or her full potential.

Chapter 7:

Body-Mind Activities

Different practices allow for the establishment of a harmonious relationship between the body and mind, such as yoga and mindfulness meditation. These mind-body activities have been proven to regulate dopamine levels in a subtle yet notable manner. When immersing oneself in flowing postures or sinking into introspective stillness, the body releases the appropriate neurotransmitters.

Strengthening connections in the brain's reward circuitry is a key benefit that can be induced by practicing various disciplines. These changes positively impact brain structure and function, which ultimately influence dopamine receptor production and sensitivity. Meditation, specifically, has been proven to result in better dopamine regulation and may be an effective way to enhance the brain's reward system.

Mind-body practices have been noted to produce a profound sense of contentment and fulfillment that is not fleeting or unsatisfactory through the stimulated release of dopamine. While sugary sweets and online social interactions produce quick dopamine boosts, these practices create a more long-lasting and purposeful connection with the neurotransmitter. This can reduce the urge for external rewards and improve emotional balance. By cultivating an even-minded and bodily-centered outlook, mind-body practices may ease the relentless search for immediate pleasure.

As with any scientific debate, caution is expressed by some. These skeptics claim that the connection between mind-body movements and dopamine is not completely understood, and its results could differ across individuals. Additionally, doubts are raised as to whether the tranquility and equilibrium induced by these practices stem solely from dopamine modulation or if other neurochemical pathways contribute significantly.

With regard to the evolving subject of dopamine regulation and mind-body activities, there appears to be a fascinating and hopeful connection that is being gathered. It is believed that beyond simply providing a momentary escape from life's chaos, these practices could have a long-lasting influence on our dopamine association.

Mindfulness

New applications of this ancient methodology have emerged, especially concerning the management of dopamine levels in modern times.

Through various techniques like mindfulness, we can steady our ever-changing thoughts and emotions. By becoming aware of our current environment, sensations, or breath, we can break free from the erratic ups and downs of dopamine. Making room for conscious observation, we can step back from our impulses and examine them with clarity.

Through conscious management of our focus and heightened awareness of the present, we establish equilibrium between ourselves and the incentives at hand. Progressively, our involuntary responses are replaced by a mindful approach. By acting as a blockade, mindfulness strategies redirect dopamine toward smoother waters, guarding against an overflow within our neural pathways.

Our relationship with emotions becomes more authentic when mindfulness is practiced. Rather than seeking immediate satisfaction, it prioritizes present experience. The worry that stems from fixations on the future or remorse from the past vanishes in the tranquility of the present. With the ability to view our thoughts without prejudice and acknowledge our sensations without opposition, stress unravels its tight grasp.

The journey of practicing mindfulness is one that demands commitment and persistence. The restless nature of the mind, always seeking novel experiences, can often put up a fight against the idea of focusing one's attention. However, with perseverance, our ability to intentionally direct our attention improves, much like a developed muscle. The rewards of this exertion are manifold—beyond just having a calming effect on dopamine, mindfulness also enhances our brain's flexibility, nurtures emotional regulation, and boosts mental fortitude.

Meditation

Meditative practices can influence dopamine pathways, slowing the need for instant gratification and fostering a more mindful relationship with our emotions.

In addition, meditation can reconfigure the sensitivity of dopaminergic receptors, those molecular gatekeepers that determine how we interpret and react to dopamine. Consistent practice seems to fine-tune these receptors, creating a more harmonious tuning in our brain's response to the chemical stream. This recalibration can enhance our ability to experience genuine pleasure in small things, defying the tyranny of constantly seeking external stimuli.

As we fine-tune our relationship with dopamine, we also cultivate the aptitude to observe our emotions without judgment, embracing even the most turbulent ones with equanimity.

Mental clarity, meanwhile, emerges like the serene river flowing through a clear forest. Meditation, by shaping the release and perception of dopamine, can help dispel mental fog and foster cognitive acuity. Mental noise gives way, making room for a lucidity that extends beyond the practice itself, weaving itself into the fabrics of our daily decisions.

A Guide for Starters

Although the process may initially seem abstruse, with proper guidance and patience, the beginner can unravel the riddles of meditation with surprising fluency.

In taking the first steps on this introspective path, one should first select a quiet corner where distractions are minimized, and the atmosphere promotes stillness. Silence, that symphony of peace, is an ideal companion on this journey. Physical comfort, often underestimated, becomes the foundation upon which the meditative experience is built. The posture, whether sitting with dignity on a cushion or lying with awareness on a flat surface, should be held with gentleness but firmness.

Breathing is the critical starting point. Observing the rhythmic flow of the breath, like waves caressing the shore, provides a secure anchorage for a mind that yearns to wander. You can imagine your breath as beach waves and synchronize the inhalation and exhalation with that illustration. However, this is no easy task. Thoughts, intrepid wanderers, can defy control, attempting to hijack attention. Herein lies the challenging beauty of meditation: like a gentle but persistent coach, we are asked to gently redirect our awareness to the breath whenever our mind wanders.

In the range of meditative techniques, mindfulness practice and concentration stand out as succulent options. In the former, we become equanimous observers of every thought, sensation, or emotion that arrives in our consciousness without judgment or attachment. The mind, like an immaculate mirror, reflects reality in its pure state. In concentration, we focus our attention on a single point of focus, whether it is the flickering of a candle or a resonant mantra. Like a refined craftsman, we train the mind to remain unwavering, defying the jumble of thoughts that seeks to erode our concentration.

Perseverance in this meditative journey is vitally important. Like any art or discipline, the fruits ripen slowly but surely. As the weeks and months pass, the benefits unfold. A sharper mental clarity emerges, allowing one to approach daily challenges with renewed calm. Answers to inner questions, hidden behind the din of modern life, bubble up like springs in a hidden oasis.

Yoga

The physical positions and postures practiced in this discipline are called asanas. The purpose of these postures is to enhance physical health with flexibility, strength, and balance. For mental health, these postures help promote concentration and calmness.

In the practice of yoga, there are a wide variety of asanas, each with its own unique characteristics and benefits. These postures can range from standing, seated, lying, or inverted positions. Some asanas are more challenging and require greater flexibility or strength, while others are more relaxing and designed to calm the mind.

Yoga, in its multi-layered nature, nourishes these dopaminergic pathways from multiple angles. The physical component of yoga, exemplified in asanas that challenge body strength and flexibility, has been shown to trigger dopamine release. By activating muscle fibers and stimulating motor neural circuits, regular asana practice promotes sustained dopamine release, nurturing a sense of satisfaction and well-being.

However, yoga transcends the mere domain of the physical. Its mental dimension, crystallized in conscious breathing and meditation techniques, also contributes to the regulation of dopaminergic pathways. Deep, conscious breathing, a cornerstone of yoga, influences the autonomic nervous system, modulating the stress response and thereby indirectly regulating dopamine release. By synchronizing movement, breathing, and mindfulness, yoga harmonizes internal energy currents, promoting the smooth circulation of dopamine.

Tips to Start

The enthralling realm of yoga as a novice can seem like quite the obstacle course, but it's a singular chance to discover how the body and mind converge through an age-old custom. Yoga, which derives from early India, has progressed into a worldwide regimen that strives to even out bodily power with inner calmness.

Embarking on the journey of yoga requires cultivating the right mindset, one that encompasses more than just asanas. This introspective journey leads to greater self-awareness and a deeper connection with the present moment. Growth on this path requires humility and patience, but the rewards are invaluable.

A competent teacher can make all the difference in this yogic journey. Core values of yoga, like self-discipline (tapas) and nonviolence (ahimsa), are not only taught but instilled by skilled instructors who guide precise postures. These principles, based on yogic philosophy, deepen understanding of the practice. A good starting point, if you can't find an instructor, are platforms like *YouTube* or apps like *Yoga for Beginners*. They provide many different routines and detailed instructions. To ensure proper performance of asanas, consider using a mirror as you practice individual postures.

Each variation of yoga type offers a unique experience, making it bewildering for beginners to choose. The dynamism of Vinyasa and the meticulousness of Iyengar are just two of the available styles. If you're starting out, it's best to begin with Hatha Yoga, which offers a leisurely introduction to yoga, allowing you to familiarize yourself with the basic postures and conscious breathing.

Providing a steady flow of oxygen to the body and promoting mental calm, breathing is a fundamental pillar of yoga practice. Nurturing the very essence of yoga, mindfulness of the breath during practice strengthens the bond between body and mind. Significant benefits can be achieved through learning proper breathing techniques.

Comfort is key when it comes to clothing and equipment in the world of yoga. If you want to achieve a full range of movement, stretchy and breathable attire is the go-to pick. For stability during the postures, a non-slip mat is essential. Slow and steady wins the race, so bear in mind that progress and growth take time. Otherwise, feelings of irritation and exasperation can result. Always keep this advice in mind, as yoga can be molded to fit any skill level.

Pilates

In essence, Pilates allows progress toward improved postural hygiene that is integrated into daily life. Deliberate movements, executed with meticulous attention, become the foundation for supreme coordination.

The masterful fusion of breath awareness and body alignment propels a seismic shift in muscle toning. Each inhalation of activated muscles and each exhalation is an opportunity to release superfluous tensions. The deep muscles, usually relegated to the shadows, emerge as major players in this body-sculpting narrative.

The wonder of Pilates lies in its power to adapt to various levels of physical and mental fitness. From cautious novices to accomplished athletes, the method molds itself, gradually but relentlessly challenging. Through conscious repetition, movement patterns are refined, strength is magnified, and agility becomes a treasure within reach.

Easy to Start

The harmonious union of body and mind is the focus of practicing Pilates, which can be done seamlessly in the comfort of your own home. Exercise is an excellent way to merge serenity with your personal environment. Even though the method may seem difficult initially, fluency and dexterity will develop with consistent practice.

Find an area in your home that is large and quiet. A quality, cushioning, and supportive mat will be your traveling companion on this journey to body alignment. If you wish to delve into more advanced variations, elements such as Pilates balls, elastic bands, and hoops can enrich your repertoire.

The sequence of exercises in Pilates embraces a symphony of fluid and conscious movements. From the foundation, the "hundred" awakens vitality in your abdominal muscles as you keep your legs up and arms pumping gracefully. This initial compass paves the way for postures like the "plank," where stability and strength meet in a delicate balance. The "cobra," with its graceful spinal extension, awakens the flexibility of the back, while the "swan dive" adds a dynamic component that tones the lumbar region. We suggest for further illustration to investigate independently what these exercises should look like.

As you progress on your Pilates at-home journey, the art of breathing becomes a mainstay. Deep inhalation and controlled exhalation synchronize with the fluidity of your movements, bringing a meditative approach that caresses both body and mind. Transitions between exercises, those seemingly silent connections, reveal grace in movement and control over every muscle involved.

The progression in Pilates is a constantly evolving canvas. From fundamental postures to advanced variations, each session pushes you beyond your previous limits. The "roll up" deploys spinal flexion with gravity-defying elegance, while the "teaser" encapsulates the harmony between strength and balance. The "hundred on the chair" or the "side leg springs" can introduce you to a dimension of resistance through apparatus, should you choose to explore beyond the mat.

Self-Awareness and Emotional Regulation

The foundation upon which emotional intelligence is built is formed by the intertwined skills of self-awareness and emotional regulation, necessary for personal growth through the search for self-reflection. Embarking on this introspective journey may frighten most people, and few feel prepared for it.

Physical and mental harmony converge in body-mind exercises, becoming a haven where self-awareness blossoms and emotional intelligence flourishes. Mastering yoga or meditation lays down the stepping stones for a dialogue between the body and soul that hones in on internal bodily cues. Developing this intuitive communication unlocks a profound comprehension of one's own sentiments and sensations, fostering a strong cornerstone of self-awareness.

Breathing consciously is the most effective way to unlock inner peace and enhance self-awareness, which is integral to mastering mind-body practices. This process also helps regulate emotions, enabling individuals to control their impulsive reactions. By gaining a greater level of command over their breath, individuals can view their emotions from a more detached viewpoint. This perspective allows them to respond rather than react impulsively to difficult scenarios.

Through such practices, self-awareness flowers and yields numerous rewards across different spheres of life. When it comes to decision-making, introspection brings about matchless lucidity. By comprehending our subconscious drives and emotional inclinations, we become better enabled to select options that resonate with our ideals and aspirations. Self-awareness imbues us with a sagacious perceptiveness that peels away external pressures and paves the way for genuine and mindful choices.

Nurture your tranquility by honing your self-awareness in the battle against stress. Early recognition of stress helps us stop it before it overtakes us. The ability to modulate stress responses and cultivate resilience comes from impartial observation of our emotional state. Self-awareness acts as a shield against stress accumulating beyond control, but it also provides wisdom to safeguard our inner peace.

Resilience and Mental Flexibility

Cultivating resilience and mental flexibility have become vital skills for navigating psychologically, ultimately strengthening our ability to tackle daily challenges. True mastery of shaping an adaptable and unyielding mindset arises from actively engaging in activities that embrace these dimensions. Emerging as invaluable traits of humanity, honing these strings is key.

It takes a lot of courage to approach life's unpredictability with a calm and serene attitude. However, one can achieve this through their ability to adapt their thoughts, emotions, and perceptions to new encounters, coupled with their resilience in the face of adversity. These traits not only arm us to confront difficulties headfirst, but they also aid in gracefully maneuvering through life's unexpected hurdles, affording us opportunities to develop and evolve.

To boost mental flexibility, these physical activities that involve mental exercises are a smart choice. Among them, yoga, mindfulness, and meditation offer an exceptional blend. During yoga practice, individuals develop the skill of acknowledging their mind and body's boundaries in a non-judgmental way. Meanwhile, mindfulness and meditation teach people how to neutrally observe their thoughts and feelings, devoid of any attachments. This newfound skill enables one to modify thoughts and emotions that restrain them.

Navigating through uncertainties with ease requires an agile way of thinking, which is fundamental to personal and societal progress. Effective leadership and strong communities that can overcome adversity are cultivated by this mindset. The ability to turn obstacles into opportunities is essential for growth and resilience. It's not just about persevering; it's about embracing diverse perspectives to find creative solutions for any situation.

Chapter 8:

Nourishing the Brain

In collaboration, vital nutrients regulate dopamine synthesis and sustain its optimal neurochemical balance in the brain.

Essential amino acids are fundamental components that our body isn't capable of creating independently. Precursors of dopamine, phenylalanine, and tyrosine are two of these amino acids that are exceptionally valuable. Initially, phenylalanine, which is discovered in lean meats, fish, and dairy products, is the starting point. With the help of the phenylalanine hydroxylase enzyme and co-factors like iron and vitamin C, this substance is converted into tyrosine.

In the hunt for protein-rich edibles, tyrosine can be hunted down in choices such as eggs, legumes, fish, poultry, and dairy products. Despite tyrosine's presence, pyridoxine, which is also known as vitamin B6, is the key to dopamine production. Without this handy cofactor, converting the tyrosine cannot occur, which is a fundamental step in the dopamine synthesis pathway. This domino effect means that pyridoxine's presence is vital. Nuts, lean meats, and whole grains offer an array of sources for acquiring vitamin B6.

The process of converting thyroxine to dopamine hinges on the presence of vital enzyme cofactors iron and magnesium. Neurons require trace minerals for this transformation to occur, as they create the underlying conditions necessary for the process to happen. Iron is the driving force behind the enzyme's catalyzation, absorbing from a range of dietary sources such as seafood, legumes, and red meat.

Folic acid, a part of the B vitamin network, can be found in fortified cereals, green leafy vegetables, and legumes. Vitamin B9, also known as folic acid, is vital to the smooth operation of the nervous system and supports the creation of dopamine through amino acid metabolism. The unique, interdependent roles of B vitamins ensure that our nutritional requirements are met.

Fatty Acids

Dopamine receptor sensitivity is kept in good shape by these polyunsaturated fatty acids, which have been found to be linked to the membrane of nerve cells.

In the web of neurotransmitter communication, where do omega-3s fit? Their contribution is interlaced with the crosshatch of the cell membrane, which results in its flexibility and adaptability. This agility is fundamental for dopamine receptors to secure their precarious tendrils in the membrane and interpret signals accurately. A wealth of omega-3s streamlines the membrane to guide dopamine-receptor interaction with finesse. Nevertheless, omega-3 insufficiency dampens its capacity, thus downgrading receptor stimulation and resulting in dopaminergic frailty commonly seen in mental health issues like depression and schizophrenia.

The availability of omega-3 fatty acids is largely dependent on one's diet and can be obtained fortuitously through the consumption of fatty fish. Genuine fortresses in returning the essential molecules necessary for health to our diet; salmon and herring swim and accumulate these fish-specific omega-3 fatty acids. Plated for consumption, their tissues deliver the necessary dosage once in our hands. The vegetable gems known as flax seeds also offer a variety of omega-3s, specifically alpha-linolenic acid. It must be noted, though, that these omega-3s found in plants require a further step to change into docosahexaenoic acid (DHA), which is the preferred form for brain health.

Playing a vital role in the cognitive and emotional domains, omega-3s extend their influence beyond the limitations of the body. These nutrients have the potential to regulate cognitive function and mood, thus becoming valuable allies of the mind, which is a constantly changing canvas of emotions and thoughts. Research suggests that a balanced intake of omega-3s could help to maintain cognitive abilities and alleviate depressive symptoms over time. While the precise impact of these fatty acids remains a mystery, there are hypotheses that indicate that optimizing dopamine receptor function may be one of the ways in which omega-3s benefit our nutrition.

Antioxidants

Antioxidants, armed with their molecular diversity and chemical prowess, do important work deep in the brain. Their main function is to neutralize free radicals, unstable molecules that form naturally during metabolic processes and which, in excess, can generate molecular chaos that damages neuronal cells. Dopaminergic neurons, producers of the essential dopamine, are particularly susceptible to this oxidative stress due to their high energy demand and constant production of reactive by-products.

Imagine antioxidants as an impenetrable shield enveloping these neurons, deftly deactivating the free radicals lurking around them. Compounds like vitamin C, vitamin E, and glutathione dive into the fray, offering stable electrons to calm the molecular storms. This chemical interaction preserves the integrity of dopaminergic neurons, extending their lifespan and contributing to cognitive and motor health.

The bravery of antioxidants is not limited to a single act; their presence in the brain extends across diverse regions, providing comprehensive support for brain health. In addition to protecting dopamine-producing neurons, antioxidants participate in regulating cerebral blood flow, promoting an optimal environment for metabolism and neuronal function. This balance enriches brain plasticity, enabling adaptations and lifelong learning.

Their influence extends to glial cells, the silent guardians that nourish and sustain neurons in their delicate electrical work. In addition, antioxidants participate in intercellular communication, modulating the release of neurotransmitters and key molecules for brain function.

Protein Quality

Proteins, constructed of chains of amino acids interconnected in specific ways, are the essential building blocks for the synthesis and maintenance of neurotransmitters such as dopamine. Feeding the brain with a diverse range of amino acids is crucial, as these compounds are the precursors of key neurotransmitters, including dopamine.

Adequate protein intake is essential to provide the body with essential amino acids, those that our body cannot synthesize and must be obtained through the diet. Such intake is a critical determinant in the availability of precursors for the production of essential neurotransmitters. Animal protein sources, such as lean meat, dairy, and eggs, have more complete and balanced amino acid profiles, supplying all the building blocks required for optimal neurotransmitter synthesis.

The role of vegetable protein sources should not be underestimated. Although they present less complete amino acid profiles compared to animal sources, the strategic combination of different plant sources can achieve adequate essential amino acid intake. Legumes, nuts, whole grains, and soy products, for example, can be combined to make up for mutual deficiencies and form an equitable amino acid repertoire.

In this environment of neurochemical interdependence, dietary variability is of paramount importance. The diversification of protein sources, both animal and vegetable, not only guarantees the acquisition of essential amino acids but also favors the richness of other coadjuvant nutrients, such as B vitamins and minerals. This holistic approach stands as an essential link in the chain linking protein quality to healthy dopaminergic function.

A Balanced Diet

In this brain diet, brightly colored fruits and vegetables are the stars of the show, offering antioxidants that clear the way for crisp, clear cognitive functioning.

We can't leave out carbohydrates, the energizers of the bunch. Like dancers keeping a steady beat, complex carbohydrates provide a steady supply of glucose, the brain's primary source of energy. Opting for whole grains and legumes is like ensuring optimal brain function.

Regular intervals between meals allow the body and brain to replenish and recalibrate. Intermittent fasting, an intriguing practice, seems to perform a deep cleansing and regenerative cleansing, eliminating excess cellular waste and allowing the brain to breathe easily.

Mindful Eating

As we move into mindful eating, we must skillfully weigh the foods that will star in our nutritional journey to promote optimal brain health. Imagine this culinary odyssey as a precision task, where variability and proportion are key.

Abundant in fatty fish such as salmon and sardines, these memory and learning artists deserve a prominent place on the daily menu. Likewise, walnuts and chia seeds, daring acrobats of brain health, provide an essential dose of these stellar nutrients.

The plant-based protagonists of this narrative, vibrantly pigmented fruits and vegetables, are like gems in the crown of brain nutrition. Blueberries, for example, rich in antioxidants, clear the stage for an aging-resistant brain. Meanwhile, spinach and broccoli, true green warriors, provide folate and vitamin K, essential nutrients for cognitive function that you won't want to leave out of your daily diet.

On the protein scene, foods that can be on our table every day are legumes and whole grains, which claim their place as prominent players. Lentils and quinoa, masters of energy sustainability, provide the brain with a steady stream of glucose, maintaining mental alertness throughout the day. Lean fish, such as cod and sole, are rich in vitamin B12, a key vitamin for nervous system health.

The interplay of vitamins and minerals is the harmonious chorus that accompanies these protagonists. Magnesium, a multifaceted virtuoso present in walnuts and spinach, promotes relaxation and brain plasticity.

B vitamins, found in lean meats, eggs, and dairy products, sing a hymn to brain metabolism. In case some of these foods are absent in your diet, it is suggested to opt for mineral or vitamin supplementation depending on the food group or food that is absent.

We should not ignore the essential role of adequate amounts. As managers of our nutritional diet, we must administer moderate portions so as not to overshadow brain work with excesses. Diversity is our ally, but moderation is the master key to maintaining lasting nutritional harmony. In this culinary narrative, the magic is in the mix and proportion, in judicious choice, and in the right measure.

Blood Sugar Regulation

Blood glucose levels play a central role in the body's metabolic machinery. These levels, largely determined by the nature of our meals, impact not only the immediate energy they supply but also the brain's dopamine-led reward machinery. A spike in sugar levels resulting from a binge of refined carbohydrates can trigger a surge of dopamine, that molecule of gratification that splashes shades of pleasure in our brains.

However, this link between carbohydrates and dopamine is more subtle than just a hedonistic indulgence. Carbohydrates come in several forms: refined, rapidly assimilated carbohydrates and complex carbohydrates, which unfold gradually in the bloodstream. The former, with their abrupt and ephemeral entry, can lead to a series of emotional ups and downs. These refined carbohydrates are well known and adored by the palate for their taste and texture but must be moderated and restricted to take care of our brains and emotions.

Examples of refined carbohydrates include white flour, obtained by grinding cereal grains such as wheat and removing the bran and germ, and white sugar, extracted from sugar cane or beets and refined to remove impurities and minerals. Other examples are white rice, obtained by peeling and polishing brown rice, and white pasta, made from white wheat flour. In addition, many processed foods, such as cookies, cakes, and sugary cereals, also contain refined carbohydrates in the form of flour and added sugars.

In terms of the brain's reward center, complex carbohydrates are essentially a soothing agent. They're distributed in measured quantities, which helps stave off the kind of sugar fluctuations that can mess with our emotional state. A variety of whole grains, legumes, and veggies contain these vital compounds, which foster physical and emotional well-being alongside a steady stream of dopamine in our neural circuitry.

Complex carbohydrates can be exemplified by whole grains, complete with their fiber- and nutrient-dense husks. Brown rice, oats, quinoa, whole wheat, barley, and whole grain bread all count. Legumes, too, provide copious complex carbs, as chickpeas, beans, peas, and lentils harness protein, fiber, and vital nutrients.

Potatoes, sweet potatoes, carrots, and pumpkins are considered starchy vegetables that contain complex carbohydrates and beneficial nutrients for overall health. Meanwhile, fruits contain natural sugars but also harbor a remarkable amount of fiber and other nutrients that can inhibit carbohydrate absorption. An array of fruits such as apples, pears, berries, and citrus fruits possess complex carbohydrates that make them an excellent carbohydrate source.

Dairy products, such as milk, house lactose in the guise of carbohydrates. Lactose, being a simple carbohydrate, remains present in dairy products. The incorporation of protein and fat in such products can hinder lactose absorption, resulting in a comparable effect to complex carbohydrates.

Opting for a plate brimming with refined carbohydrates can offer a momentary passport to euphoria, but it can also leave us shipwrecked in the turbulent waters of anxiety and irritability. In contrast, a thoughtful selection of complex carbohydrates brings with it a more enduring promise: that of stable dopamine, a serene mood, and a mind that navigates solidly through the swell of circumstance. These can be more present in the daily diet in combination with other foods to increase the amount of plant fiber on the plate.

The Gut-Brain Connection

Dwelling at the very core of this mesmerizing interplay is the assortment of microorganisms that reside in our intestines, popularly known as the gut microbiota. Acting as more than just the digesters of food, their sway over our well-being expands to encompass even the mental and cognitive domains. Of all these intriguing revelations, the most notable one is the unbreakable bond between dopamine production and the gut microbiota.

The microbiota, like a microscopic conductor, indirectly regulates dopamine production through various pathways. It influences the availability of precursors necessary for dopamine synthesis. But that's not where their role ends; these tiny companies also participate in the regulation of gene expression associated with dopamine production, thus affecting its balance in the brain.

This is where prebiotics, probiotics, and dietary fiber come into play as the secondary players in this narrative. Prebiotics, the nutrients that nourish beneficial bacteria, act as the fuel for the growth and activity of bacteria that can positively influence dopamine production. Probiotics, meanwhile, are the selected microbial strains that can support gut health and modulate gut-brain communication, which may indirectly influence dopamine.

Dietary fiber acts as a kind of architect, building the physical structure for beneficial bacteria to flourish in the gut. This robust gut ecology, in turn, can have an impact on dopamine production and regulation.

Our ever-expanding understanding of this gut-brain connection invites us to explore new avenues of intervention, ranging from optimizing our diet to nourish the microbiota to considering personalized probiotic therapies.

Possible Healthy Diets

If you don't want to go to a nutritionist or a doctor to elaborate on a diet with the nutritional requirements covered for brain and gut health, there are some preexisting popular diets you can consider.

Mediterranean Diet

The Mediterranean diet, revered for its exquisiteness and sustenance in authentic flavors, shines as a culinary treasure that reverberates in cerebral and enteric well-being.

The profound relationship between the Mediterranean diet and brain wellness emanates from its rich source of antioxidants, polyphenols, and essential fatty acids. Vibrant green leafy vegetables, juicy seasonal fruits, and golden olive oils converge in an interplay that nourishes brain cells and protects against the siege of free radicals, thus preserving cognitive acuity and delaying neuronal deterioration.

In parallel, the culinary song of the Mediterranean resounds in the intestinal corridors, where the balance of the microbiota finds its optimum. Prebiotic fiber, rooted in whole grains and legumes, fertilizes the intestinal terrain to cultivate a diverse and healthy flora. This combination of foods, guided by the compass of fermentation, not only promotes harmonious digestion but also nurtures a symbiotic relationship between the gut and the brain, by virtue of the gut-brain connection.

It is pertinent to underline that the Mediterranean diet transcends the mere physical, reaching the very essence of socialization and culinary appreciation. Feasts shared around tables laden with delicacies not only nourish the body but also nourish the soul and stimulate the production of hormones that induce satisfaction and emotional well-being.

Nordic Diet

Based on the conventional eating habits of Scandinavian communities, the Nordic diet is known for its ability to tantalize your taste buds while also providing numerous advantages for both your gut and brain health. A plethora of benefits that go beyond just food but rather contribute to your general well-being.

Promoting mental sharpness and cognitive clarity requires a foundation of omega-3-rich foods like salmon and herring, known to be anti-inflammatory and supportive of neuron communication. Wild berries such as raspberries and blueberries add a burst of antioxidants to combat oxidative stress—a proven culprit of neurodegenerative disease.

Cruciferous vegetables, such as the trusty broccoli and mighty kale, are the major players in this dietary scheme and boast plentiful prebiotic fibers that are absolutely essential for keeping the gut microbiota alive and well. Delicate whole grains like oats and barley round out this vibrant spread, furnishing a tasty contrast and also lending fibers that prop up the immune system and fortify the blood-brain barrier. By carefully balancing these components, one can enjoy a truly complete and wholesome diet for optimal health.

Venture further into the wilds of Nordic cuisine and find almonds and chia, nuts and seeds providing vital nutrients like healthy fats and vitamin E, safeguarding brain cells from aging. Embark on a flavor quest with cardamom and ginger, exotic spices that also improve blood flow and calm inflammation, promoting cerebral watering and efficient vascular systems.

Chapter 9:

Restful Sleep

Additionally, in this neurochemical system that directs sleep, dopamine is a key figure in the synchronization of circadian rhythms and the regulation of the sleep-wake cycle.

In the theater of the mind, dopamine displays its masterful performance in the circadian system, setting the tempo of the internal biological clock. In harmonious tandem with other biochemical actors, this master molecule guides the rhythms of sleep and wakefulness. Dopamine, like the sun in the firmament of neurotransmitters, welcomes the dawn of wakefulness and withdraws with the elegance of sunset, making way for melatonin, the sleep hormone. This symmetrical alternation, driven by the delicate balance of dopamine, shapes the characteristics of our circadian rhythm.

Throughout the day, dopamine is also in charge, like a master of ceremonies of alertness and wakefulness. In daytime brain interaction, this neurotransmitter plays its role through a reward system, giving us the energy and attention needed to face tasks and challenges. Dopamine pulls back the curtain on the limbic system, stimulating the prefrontal cortex and enlivening attention and concentration. Thus, it stands out as the architect of our cognitive clarity, instilling mental acuity and keeping the senses on guard.

However, this play of light and shadow performed by dopamine is not without complexity. When night falls, dopamine must cede its role to melatonin, allowing restful sleep to enter the picture. But sometimes, the stars of equilibrium can swing. Imbalances in the regulation of dopamine can lead to sleep disorders, where the alteration of this neurotransmitter introduces dissonance in the score of the night's rest.

Sleep's Impact on Dopamine Production

The interaction between sleep and dopamine reveals a function in which the quality and duration of sleep play a leading role. As the night unfolds its blanket of dreams, the processes of memory consolidation and cellular restoration begin to build within sleep. However, it is the prominence of dopamine, that fearless chemical messenger, which adds a fascinating dimension.

The narrative begins with the quality of sleep: restful rest lays a red carpet of sensitivity to dopaminergic receptors. The sleep cycle system, with its slow-wave movements and rapid eye movements, synchronizes with the reward system, allowing receptors to trap dopamine signals with greater affinity. Duration, in turn, adjusts the volume of this chemical serenade: adequate sleep amplifies the dopaminergic response, intensifying the perception of pleasure and motivation.

However, this plot would not be complete without exploring the shadows that lurk when sleep deprivation enters the picture. In a twist worthy of tragedy, dopaminergic function takes a harrowing turn when sleep is impaired. The receptors, so sensitive and eager to catch dopamine signals, are dulled. Reward fades, motivation wavers, and pleasure-seeking becomes a fatiguing act. The cascade of consequences spreads through the domains of attention, decision-making, and emotional regulation, sowing the seeds of irritability and diminished cognitive performance.

Thus, in this web of neurochemistry and dreams, the function of dopamine finds its balance in the fine thread of sleep. The symbiotic relationship between the two underscores the importance of taking care of a good night's rest as an act of brain nourishment. As spectators and actors in this drama, we are faced with the conscious choice of ensuring the quality of sleep that will fine-tune dopamine receptors, sustaining motivation and cognitive well-being.

Sleep for Brain Health

During the REM (rapid eye movement) sleep phase, brain synapses undergo meticulous maintenance, a cleansing process that purges metabolic waste accumulated throughout the day, paving the way for a subsequent day of mental clarity. This nocturnal ritual not only affects the regulation of attention and concentration but also influences more sophisticated processes.

The consolidation of memory, that vital faculty that weaves the fabric of our experience, flourishes in the garden of sleep. Slowed brain waves during deep sleep phases facilitate the transfer of information from short-term memory to long-term memory. It is as if, during the night, the brain remodels the aisles of its internal library, organizing thoughts and experiences on shelves that are more resistant to forgetting. In this way, sleep not only consolidates memories but also frees mental space for new acquisitions.

No less important is the role of sleep in the subtle weaving of our emotions. The REM phase, which witnesses a maddening dance of closed eyes, is also the stage where emotional responses are rehearsed and recalibrated. During this period, the brain recreates fragments of emotional experiences, a dress rehearsal that allows the individual to process and understand their feelings. This dream therapy can be crucial for resolving emotional conflicts and cultivating psychological well-being.

However, the dream is a versatile player in the theater of the mind, playing roles that transcend the merely cognitive. The curtain rises to reveal the role of sleep in mood regulation and stress management. Chronic sleep deprivation becomes a spur to emotional vulnerability, triggering exaggerated responses to stressful situations and denting the brain's ability to regulate mood. Dreams, with their ability to replay and reinterpret the experiences of the day, provide a safe setting for processing emotional trauma and generating emotional balance.

Likewise, sleep is like a silent advisor in the decision-making conclave. Insufficient sleep translates into a loss of cognitive clarity, which impairs the ability to weigh options and make informed decisions. Brain areas involved in risk assessment and decision-making are affected by lack of sleep, which can lead to impulsive or suboptimal choices.

Ideal Sleep Duration

The question of optimal sleep time lies in varied ranges and periods, with each stage of life and each individual executing unique times. Medical wisdom has defined structures around this enigma, guiding different age groups into the territory of restful rest. Infants, like delicate butterflies, spread their dreamy wings for approximately 14-17 hours a day, a critical foundation for their developing brains. Adolescents, like night birds, need at least eight to ten hours to ensure their growth and neural maturation. The path becomes more meandering with adulthood. General guidelines advocate seven to nine hours, although each individual is a unique atlas of needs.

However, modern reality has triggered a duel between insomnia and hectic life. Electric light, that tireless ally of late hours, has blurred the boundaries between day and night. The hands of the clock run mercilessly, while adults, wrapped up in their tasks and desires, sacrifice sleep on the altar of productivity. Less sleep, that seemingly harmless act, triggers a cascade of consequences. Attention wavers like a fatigued tightrope walker, memory fragments into fragments, and emotions fluctuate like leaves in the wind.

But as in all duality, excess also lurks in the shadows. Prolonged sleep is associated with a similar cognitive decline. The nemesis of insufficient sleep manifests itself as mental sluggishness, a haze that creeps over thoughts and hinders focus. Neural connections, like abandoned trails, ambush each other in the undergrowth of inactivity.

As we navigate this tangle of drowsiness and wakefulness, balance is the captain of our cerebral ship. Ancient wisdom meets modern science, guiding us to the land of restful dreams. Adapting the bed of sleep to individual needs, adjusting the right amount to nourish the machinery of thoughts and emotions, becomes an art worthy of masters.

The Effects of Napping

On a difficult day, the siesta is like an oasis of reconstitution, where the senses meet rest and wakefulness. This lazy interlude not only offers a well-deserved respite but also triggers a chemical process in our brain, led by the stimulant dopamine. However, as in any neuronal concert, the tones are not always uniform, and the harmony is sometimes challenged by the nuances of complexity.

Naps, as episodes of daytime rest, provide a warm refuge for dopamine circuits, promoting their regulation and balance. By closing the eyelids and sinking into sleep, dopamine-releasing neurons reduce their activity, allowing the receptors to become sensitized again. It also promotes an improved mood and a greater ability to face the challenges that life presents.

However, as in any poem, there are dissonant verses. Napping, when it wanders into the territories of excess, can unleash the turbulent yoke of lethargy. Prolonged daytime sleep can alter nighttime sleep patterns and, paradoxically, affect dopamine homeostasis. An overabundance of this neurotransmitter can lead to decreased receptor sensitivity, engendering a vicious cycle of constant reward-seeking that strains emotional stability and mental clarity.

At the crossroads of time and duration, a fascinating debate unfolds. What is the optimal time to dive into dreamland and caress the dawn of dopamine? And how much should we allow ourselves to nourish our brains with the elixir of daytime rest? The answer is enigmatic and, as in the best plot, varies from individual to individual. A short nap, about 20 to 30 minutes, with just the right amount of slow—and fast—wave sleep, can stimulate dopamine and improve cognitive acuity. Meanwhile, dabbling in deeper sleep can boost creativity and problem-solving.

Creating a Sleep-Friendly Environment

In the perpetual quest for regenerative rest, the transcendental notion of sleep hygiene arises, a series of cautious practices that act as architects of an environment conducive to restorative rest. This facet, framed by holistic health, takes on an unavoidable role in optimizing the quality of sleep and, therefore, at the pinnacle of our daytime performance.

The complexities of this topic raise a large number of considerations. Among these, the transcendental influence of ambient temperature emerges. The thermoregulatory interaction of our body finds its ally in a thermally capable room, where the warm embrace of blankets intertwines with the freshness of the surrounding air. This thermal symbiosis provides the ideal environment for entering the realms of deep sleep.

Melatonin, a faithful exponent of our biological rhythms, surrenders to the charms of the twilight. In this way, the luminous glow of electronic devices or urban headlights is like the antagonist of drowsiness. The tapestry of shadows, with its elegant dexterity, thus acquires a capital role in the design of the stage where the eyes finally close their curtains.

The echoes and whispers that permeate the silence of the sunset are worthy of their weight in this nocturnal epic. Acoustic interference, like a tempest on a still lake, can blur the sharpness of repose. A chorus of distant snores or the chatter of the waking city can weave their discordant sounds into the dream. Here, cacophony becomes the antithesis of rest. The virtue of this silent compass is the mitigation of the din, the shelter of an Eden where the senses find their calm lethargy.

And in the very structure of this refuge, the mattress stands as the pedestal of sleep. Like a visionary architect, we must wisely choose the support where our dreams will rest their heads. Ergonomics and comfort are the cornerstones of this construction. A mattress with a firmness according to individual preferences, where the back finds its graceful curvature, is the salvation from the daily hustle and bustle. In this wellness capsule, the alchemy of materials and design provides the passport to the nirvana of restful sleep.

Sleep Hygiene Practices

The pre-sleep stages take on a leading role in this theater of rest. Dimming the lights and tempering the environment in warm tones, with its gentle glow, is like caressing the central nervous system, a delicate instruction to slow down its activity and prepare for retirement. Warm baths, like a watery embrace, whisper to the muscles to loosen their tensions and release their burdens. Meditation and deep breathing, in these moments of twilight, invite the mind to shed the worries of the day and embrace the calm that precedes sleep. Here, in this arena, prior to the ecstasy of rest, each act counts as a grain of sand to build the hygiene of sleep.

However, a challenging antagonist has emerged: electronic devices, with their incandescent glow of blue light. In a world where connectivity is ubiquitous, it has become tempting to plunder the night of its secrets in the sanctuary of screens. But science has warned us with a stern nuance. Blue light, that electronic nemesis, tricks the retinas by appearing to be the sun, disrupting the production of melatonin, the sleep-regulating hormone. Thus, while the digital world offers us a window to the world, it stealthily closes the curtains of our deep sleep.

The same technology that connects us can also unplug us from our most fundamental rest. The paradox is amplified by screen time, that digital currency we spend without pause. Screens, with their hypnotic flashes, rob us of precious moments of sleep. With every scroll and tap, we buy waking hours on credit, mortgaging our future rest.

Regular Sleep Schedules

Preserving our physical and mental health is crucial, and a regular sleep schedule plays a fundamental role in achieving this goal. Do not underestimate the importance of the exact synchronization between the internal biological clock and the sleep-wake cycle—it is a key process that cannot be neglected.

Amid the ceaseless stream of stimuli and cutting-edge tech, we frequently feel drawn to push past temporal restraints, trading in slumber for increased leisure or progress. Abiding by such artificial schedules inevitably results in cascading fallout across all facets of our existence.

Biological processes are linked to a predictable sleep schedule, which involves the sleep-wake cycle and the circadian clock. These processes affect not only sleep quality but also cardiovascular health, metabolism, and cognitive function. A disruption in this balance, however, can cause problems with the production of melatonin, such as chronic insomnia, daytime fatigue, and mood disorders. If explored thoroughly, one can truly understand the importance of a consistent sleep schedule.

Fostering a regular bedtime and wake-up schedule delivers considerable and enduring advantages. A steady sleep timing cultivates synchronized coordination between internal rhythms and external environmental needs, thereby enabling a more prompt and profound sleep. The coordination of these internal rhythms additionally funds greater metabolic effectiveness that can obstruct disorders like obesity and diabetes.

A consistent sleep-wake cycle forms a firm foundation for maintaining good mental health. Managing stress and effective learning are directly impacted by adequate sleep, which correlates with emotion regulation and memory consolidation. A dependable sleep schedule leads to enhancing mental clarity and mood, showcasing the tight connection between psychological well-being and a sound slumber.

Stress Management for Sleep

Stress, displaying its many facets, also acts as an unwelcome destroyer of healthy sleep habits. This intrusion is manifested in the alteration of dopamine production. In moments of prolonged stress, dopamine reserves are depleted, generating a cascade of effects that reverberate in the conciliation and quality of sleep. The inhibition of this neurotransmitter causes difficulties in reaching the deep phases of restful sleep, plunging the sleeper into a vicious cycle of chronic fatigue and accentuated stress.

At this juncture, the importance of embracing techniques that promote relaxation and temper the onslaught of stress emerges. Meditation, covered above, revered for its ability to attune mind and body, rises like a compass in this vast ocean of uncertainty. Through meditative practices, a space of serenity is established from which the individual can explore the meanderings of his or her own mind and free himself or herself from the chains of stress. Mindfulness, another jewel in this arsenal of self-regulation that we discussed earlier, nurtures the ability to immerse oneself in the present moment with an open and receptive mind, displacing the worries of the future and the regrets of the past.

However, it is in the hours before bedtime that these practices take on particular value. Adopting a bedtime routine involving meditation and mindfulness can trigger a gradual release of the day's accumulated tension. The act of setting aside time to contemplate without judgment the thoughts and emotions that visit us nurtures the ability to disconnect from the whirlwind of stress and worries, thus paving the way to a deeper, more rejuvenating sleep.

Physical Activity to Improve Sleep Quality

As we enter into this bond, the cardinal question arises: When is the ideal time to exercise so that the benefits reaped reach their zenith without disturbing the fragile balance of restful sleep?

Facing the daily battle against inert lethargy becomes more bearable when endorphins awaken the body with their energetic embrace. The courtship between physical activity and sleep runs in two directions: Exercise, through its positive influence on the architecture of sleep, promotes the consolidation of deeper and more restorative nocturnal patterns. In this way, the symbiotic relationship is forged: sleep gives the body the opportunity to regenerate and heal, while physical activity provides the ground for more revitalizing sleep.

In the theater of this vital interplay, a dilemma is revealed: when to deploy the magic of exercise to ensure its warm embrace without the shadows of fatigue disturbing the threshold of sleep? Personal chronotypes, the unique characteristics of each individual, draw divergent lines in this debate. While some find dawn the optimal time for vigorous activity, others reserve the afternoon as their peak of physical performance. Nevertheless, a consensus is on the horizon: prudence whispers that intense activity in the hours leading up to rest could interfere with the peaceful arrival of sleep. The organism requires an interval to slow down its baton before plunging into the dreamlike abyss.

Physical activity at night, although it requires moderation, does not need to be banned outright. Modalities such as yoga or stretching, delicately executed, can even be postulated as propitiatory rituals for a more serene sleep. In this journey toward an optimal balance between daytime dynamics and nocturnal stillness, self-awareness is the guide: listening to the body's own signals and discerning the subtle resonances of its rhythms carves a golden path toward harmony.

Chapter 10:

The Guide

In neuroscience, a topic of captivating relevance emerges—the importance of routines in the delicate regulation of dopamine. In the background of this fact, a phenomenon is revealed: how meticulously calculated routines can shape consistent dopaminergic responses, lending stability to the delicate neural balance.

Dopamine finds in routines a profound link. By establishing predictable patterns of activities and behaviors, the brain anticipates impending gratifications, resulting in the measured and continuous release of dopamine. This admirable phenomenon encourages the formation of healthy habits, from morning exercise to the evening ritual of unwinding. Dopamine, then, does not unfold in fiery bursts but flows in steady streams, nourishing the brain with a subtle but lasting sense of satisfaction.

Regular, predictable schedules work by providing the brain with a constant pattern, allowing for the optimization of neurotransmitter function, including dopamine. The brain, designed to seek efficiency, adapts to regularity and begins to anticipate dopamine release at specific times. This, in turn, maintains a cascade of signals that promote homeostasis, preventing excessive fluctuations that could lead to mental health problems.

The interconnection between routine and dopamine highlights how the complexity of the brain finds its counterpart in the apparent simplicity of daily habits. It is through this simplicity that the foundation for a balanced nervous system is built. However, brain plasticity also demands some variation. While regularity is crucial, excessive monotony could trigger a decrease in dopaminergic sensitivity. Therefore, it is in the conjugation of routine with moments of novelty and challenge that the nervous system finds its greatest expression of health.

Setting Clear Goals and Priorities

The journey toward success necessitates a constant pursuit of personal growth and excellence. In order to navigate toward success, it's crucial to have a clear sense of priorities and objectives to serve as a compass. To set achievable goals, one must engage in a process of strategizing, setting vantage points, and taking action.

Setting goals is like creating a roadmap for ourselves, as it directs us toward a particular destination rather than simply being a mental activity. With explicit aims, we define our course with clear signposts that indicate our direction and guide us on the path to success. As we state achievable objectives, we fortify the journey with motivation, giving ourselves an inclusive yet reasonable image of what we want to achieve.

Resources and time must be realistically considered when priorities are being set to achieve objectives that are essential for short-term growth and that build upon achievements of the future. Finding the right balance between what is possible and what is desired requires careful discernment and planning. Understanding the importance of different objectives is key to prioritizing appropriately and establishing stepping stones toward ambitious goals. This requires a deep sense of introspection and a thoughtful approach.

Our lives become imbued with a renewed sense of purpose and ambition when we establish unambiguous goals and priorities. This practical exercise enables us to seamlessly fit together each small achievement into a bigger, cohesive picture, infusing our day-to-day existence with clarity and direction. Such a heightened level of focus, in turn, acts as a catalyst for motivation, making each accomplishment a tangible indicator of progress.

Moving ahead necessitates acknowledging the likelihood that our goals may need to be adapted to accommodate shifting circumstances. Maintaining a rigid outlook could be detrimental to our prospects, but being adaptable allows us to smartly pivot and refocus our endeavors.

Structuring the Morning Routine

Meticulous planning of a morning routine highlights a cascade of psychological and physiological benefits. By bestowing a sense of purpose from the first moments of dawn, a sense of control over the day unfolding before us is strengthened. Every activity influences the mood and attitude we embrace. Establishing time-honored habits nurtures a sense of stability in a world in constant motion.

In the morning scene, a passionate debate unfolds about the inclusion of activities that incite dopamine release. The synergy between exercise, a healthy breakfast, and exposure to sunlight is a triumvirate capable of stoking the embers of our internal reward system. Early physical movement, whether in the form of a vigorous workout or a leisurely walk, triggers the release of endorphins and dopamine, stoking a sense of accomplishment and energy.

Breakfast constitutes the primary fuel for the body and brain. Choosing the right nutrients not only nourishes our cells but also impacts mood regulation and mental clarity. By choosing wisely the ingredients that make up this first culinary composition of the day, a foundation is laid for cohesion between body and mind.

Our nervous system experiences a biochemical alchemy of dopamine when sunlight interacts with our skin, inducing feelings of vitality. Vitamin D synthesis, which is essential for bone health and overall well-being, is also sparked by exposing ourselves to natural light. This exposure not only synchronizes our circadian rhythms but also acts as a catalyst for the aforementioned synthesis process.

Optimizing Work and Productivity

As we enter the fascinating realm of work optimization, it is prudent to highlight the central role played by proper task structuring. Dividing work into manageable segments, defining clear objectives, and establishing discerned priorities are fundamental pillars in this process.

By breaking down tasks into smaller units, a sharper, less overwhelming focus is fostered, allowing the individual to approach each task with renewed insight. Likewise, defining concrete goals provides a sense of incremental achievement, acting as fuel for motivation.

From Pomodoro to the GTD (getting things done) method, each approach brings its own amalgam of advantages and challenges. The famous Pomodoro method, which relies on intervals of concentrated work followed by regular breaks, may seem simple, but its impact on sustained attention and mental freshness is undeniable. However, there is a need to find the right rhythm for each individual, as the human being is not a standardized cog.

Breaks, though often underestimated, are jewels embedded in the crown of productivity. Scheduled breaks not only revive energy but also boost creativity and problem-solving by allowing the mind to wander and explore without restraint. However, the key lies in the quality of the breaks; the temptation of social media and digital distraction must be tamed diligently.

Mindfulness entails not only total immersion in the present task but also nonjudgmental recognition of intrusive thoughts. Here, the complexity lies not only in the technique itself but in the need to cultivate a deep understanding of one's own mental and emotional processes. This self-discipline not only fuels productivity but also promotes long-term psychological resilience.

Incorporating the Learnings

Integrating brief mindfulness exercises into our daily routine can be a revitalizing balm for the spirit, a necessary break in the prevailing rhythm. An initial exercise can be to dedicate a few minutes, perhaps upon waking or before going to sleep, to simply observe our breathing. With each inhalation and exhalation, the mind sheds the chains that bind it to the past and the future and plunges into the calm stream of the here and now.

But mindfulness is not limited to passive contemplation; it also involves scrutinizing our sensations and thoughts with an unbiased eye. An intermediate exercise might be "sensory exploration:" During a brief pause in the day, we are invited to pay attention to the sounds that normally go unnoticed, to the textures that lie beneath our fingertips, to the nuances of flavors in each mouthful. These everyday actions, transformed into conscious acts, take on a tinge of novelty and enrich the experience of the trivial.

On a deeper level, the practice of "mindfulness in movement" can be undertaken. Here, it is a matter of transforming a routine activity into a ritual of concentration, as if each gesture contained the grace of an ancient dance. For example, when washing the dishes, instead of letting oneself be swept away by automatism, one can concentrate on the sensation of the warm water, on the rhythmic movement of the hands, and on the pop of the bubbles.

Physical Activity

In the rhythm of life, time seems to slip through our fingers like fine sand, forging a balance between active energy and rejuvenating pause is a revitalizing habit.

The morning routine is what directs the rest of the day, the initial movement that awakens slumbering muscles and caresses the circulatory system with an invigorating caress. A yoga ritual or an early morning run awakens dopamine and embraces the day with energy. As the clock ticks down, the need for strategic breaks is a smart move. Brief interludes to stretch the arms toward the firmament or bow the neck in reverence to the ground provide refreshing relief. The complexity lies in discerning the perfect cadence: sessions that elevate the heart rate and fleeting breaks that allow for a recharge without waste.

The sinuosity of the afternoon, as the sun hovers at its zenith, summons a softer tempo. The body longs for movements that do not demand maximal deployment but caress the fatigued muscles with grace. A leisurely stroll or a few minutes of tai chi bring a warm balance to this daytime pentagram. Moments of stillness may also work. A momentary retreat to close the eyes and breathe solemnly injects serenity in the midst of the maelstrom.

Taking time to exercise with greater performance would be the way out; however, not everyone has the time and availability. In the meantime, we can take refuge in small recreational activities that demand more movement.

Balanced Nutrition

We already know that certain nutrients act as catalysts in the production and release of dopamine in the brain, thus contributing to our sense of well-being. Legumes such as beans, lentils, and chickpeas, as well as foods rich in lean proteins such as turkey, chicken, and low-fat dairy products, are excellent sources of tyrosine that deserve their place at our daily table. It is suggested to opt for these foods for lunch. Make sure that some of them are present in significant quantities.

For breakfast, we can use whole grain cereals and whole grains. For example, oatmeal is prepared in different ways and has a considerable amount of fiber. It is an excellent food and versatile for different techniques and dishes.

Nuts such as almonds, walnuts, and pumpkin seeds are nutritional treasures packed with magnesium. In addition, high-quality dark chocolate, in moderation, is not only a guilty pleasure but also a welcome source of this mineral. These foods would make excellent mid-morning or mid-afternoon snacks.

Blueberries, rich in flavonoids and spinach, packed with folic acid, are masterful examples of how nature provides us with treasures that elevate our mental well-being. The recommended fruits can be included in the diet as snacks or to complement main dishes. For example, adding blueberries to a salad.

The combination of colors and flavors in a diet that incorporates fatty fish, such as salmon, rich in omega-3 fatty acids, along with the burst of vitality offered by vitamin C-laden citrus fruits, are essential steps toward a nourished, glowing brain. Fish are excellent choices for dinner, combined with a variety of vegetables.

Digital Detox and Mindfulness

The first step to rediscovering a healthy balance between ourselves and technology is to become fully aware of our digital consumption. Reflecting on how we use our screen time is essential. A frank self-assessment will allow us to discern between productive use and mere digital escapism. Once this clarity is achieved, we can draw concrete boundaries for our online interactions.

A digital detox does not imply a total break with technology but rather a recalibration of our relationship with it. Cultivating hobbies that nurture our creativity and concentration is a powerful vehicle toward disconnection. Analog photography, gardening, or oil painting are activities that demand our full attention, dispelling electronic distractions. They also allow a reunion with patience, a quality forgotten in the fast-paced digital world. We can establish two to three days during the week to practice these pastimes after work and limit the technologies at least one hour before bedtime.

Incorporating periods of meditation and mindfulness into our daily routine is also a balm for our hectic, digitized mind. These quiet moments challenge us to savor the present, disconnecting us from the virtual anxieties that often plague us. Mindful breathing and a focus on the senses anchor us in the here and now, a haven of serenity in a sea of blinking notifications. Taking 10 minutes in the evening routine to meditate or relax the mind will go a long way.

Strategically planning "digital detox" days can provide time away from the technological spectrum. These days are characterized by outdoor adventures, face-to-face interactions, and reading paper books, rescuing the tactile pleasure of the pages between our fingers. Freed from the digital yoke, we find ourselves immersed in the whisper of the wind, the murmur of uninterrupted conversations, and the rich texture of printed words. We can choose weekends that fit our responsibilities to take trips that disconnect our senses from technology or, at home, reformulate the activities to be done on the weekend to rest from the blue light.

Sleep Hygiene

A cardinal premise in the quest for regenerative sleep is to establish a consistent routine, where the body and mind, like synchronized clocks, immerse themselves in sleep on the same schedule every night. This internal synchronization, known as circadian rhythm, is strengthened when we maintain a consistent bedtime and wake-up schedule, even on days off. This constant commitment fosters regularity, which in turn educates our body about when it is appropriate to relax its energies. According to your routine and responsibilities, establish a set bedtime and wake-up time that you can maintain even outside of work days.

Darkness, like a protective blanket, stimulates the production of melatonin, the hormone that induces sleep and becomes the primary ally of effective sleep hygiene. In this context, the gradual reduction of exposure to electronic devices before bedtime is essential. Set your sleep schedule according to your time of disconnection from electronics with two hours in between, and perform the remaining activities prior to rest with dim light.

Moderation in the intake of food and liquids before bedtime avoids digestive discomfort and nighttime trips to the bathroom, avoiding breaks in the sleep cycle. Make sure not to eat in abundance just before going to sleep.

Conclusion

Wake up, restless and curious minds! The time has come to embark on a journey toward optimizing our mental faculties and unlocking our dopamine production. In an ever-evolving world where agitation and overstimulation threaten to undermine our brain health, it is necessary to take the helm and navigate toward clarity and focus.

Imagine your brains as the most sophisticated machines whose gears and circuits need constant maintenance. As we move forward on this journey, we must embrace the variety of strategies that have the power to enliven our neural connections and nurture our cognitive functions. It's not just about adopting a passive mindset but about diving headfirst into the experience of redefining our relationship with information and learning!

Here we are, with a variety of tips that awaken curiosity and stimulate the intellect. Reading, the timeless jewel of mental exploration, is one of our most powerful weapons. From poetry that caresses the senses to treatises that challenge our perspectives, every page read is a touch with wisdom that fuels creativity and forges new connections in the labyrinth of our minds.

But that's not all! The mind craves challenges that make it vibrate and grow. Take advantage of puzzles and riddles, those challenges that make the intellectual heartthrob. By solving these puzzles, we not only strengthen our mental acuity but also release that heavenly reward known as dopamine. This neurochemical wraps us in a warm blanket of satisfaction and propels us to new cognitive heights.

Don't underestimate the power of movement, dear readers—the body in motion is the tune that wakes up the neurons! From a morning walk to a passionate dance, physical exercise pumps fresh oxygen to the brain and encourages neuronal growth. And yes, as we should know! It also triggers that wonderful dopamine, igniting the euphoria of achievement and motivation.

In this modern world full of distractions and constant noise, mindfulness becomes our most precious amulet. Don't forget to practice mindfulness, whether through serene meditation or complete immersion in a task; it allows us to tame the mental maelstrom and cultivate clarity. Remember that by tuning our senses to the present, we not only stimulate dopamine production but also create a space for introspection and self-discovery, laying the foundation for deep and lasting personal growth.

In this quest for a mind at its peak, let's never forget the magic of rest. Deep sleep is the restorer of depleted brain cells, the time when memories are consolidated, and problems find hidden solutions. Do not sacrifice this sanctuary of regeneration for the sake of an ever-evolving society that does not value your sacrifice of putting your health at risk for a little more consumption.

So, my fellow mental explorers, here I urge you to embrace this advice with fervor and joy. Embark on the path of voracious reading, challenge your brains with clever riddles, allow your bodies to dance to the rhythm of life, and grant your minds the sacred rest they deserve. The reward will be a sharp mind, revitalized dopamine production, and an unforgettable journey to cerebral excellence. Onward to the wonder of mental self-realization!

The End

At the culmination of this scientific and holistic odyssey we have undertaken throughout these pages, there is an undeniably resonant conclusion: the plasticity of our neurochemical system, particularly the dopaminergic system, reveals itself as a portal to the renewal and empowerment of our existence. In a world where the speed of modern life often challenges our capacity for biological adaptation, we discover that the pathways of wisely selected nutrition, holistic health, restful sleep, and cultivated mindfulness masterfully intertwine in interaction, delineating the pathway to the restoration and flourishing of our brain and emotional health.

In retrospect, our forays into the realm of dopamine have conferred a new appreciation for the delicately intertwined interconnection between body and mind, an eloquent reminder that we are tissues not only of cells but also of experiences and environments. Dopamine, that chemical messenger linked to pleasure and motivation, is the central player in the story of how we approach the challenge of optimizing our own biology.

As we explore the vast plains of nutrition, from crucial micronutrients to protective antioxidants, a palette of flavors and colors is revealed that transcends the mere act of nourishment and takes on the dimension of a tool for conscious self-affirmation. The epiphany lies in the informed choice of foods that nourish both our body and mind, creating a harmonious balance that reverberates in every neural impulse.

In tune with this wellness system, the wholeness of health is a guiding beacon in our journey toward dopaminergic recovery. The exercises that nourish our heart also reverberate in the regions that house our brain reward, a tangible testament to how biology responds to investment in its own care. Sleep, that nightly rest of regeneration, is a fundamental pillar where the harmonization of circadian rhythms triggers cascades of cellular and neural renewal.

In this apogee of reflection, mindfulness stands as the crown jewel in this journey toward self-regulation. The diligent and consistent practice of being fully present in every inhale and exhale, in every beat and whisper of thought, manifests as the alchemy that transcends the sum of its parts. In the stillness of mindfulness, we find the key to unraveling the threads of compulsion and addiction, to freeing ourselves from the invisible chains that bind us to obsolete patterns.

Ultimately, this volume summons us to a retreat of introspection and action, a performance in which every nutritional choice, every heartbeat of exercise, every minute of sleep, and every moment of mindful presence come together in a harmonious chorus of self-restoration. As we close this theme, the promise and potential to reconfigure our own physiology and psychology unfolds before us like a gift waiting to be unpacked. The direction toward dopaminergic recalibration, and thus toward a life of greater wholeness and authenticity, is now a map unfolding before us. It is up to us to follow it with determination, with gratitude, and with the certainty that we are the artisans of our own neurological and emotional renewal.

You can restart and reprogram your biological function with the best guidance through this book. It's in your hands to become the healthiest version of yourself today!

About the Author

Ameri Dacre is a dedicated and compassionate advocate for mental health and the correlation it has with our physical health, working closely with neuroscience.

She earned her master's as a psychotherapist with a background of working in NICU, Ameri has witnessed the transformative power and the profound impact that proper sleep, nutrition, and brain health can have on individuals from an early age. Having a family herself, she prioritizes her family's health and wellness.

Combining her expertise in neuroscience, Ameri has spent years researching and understanding the intricate connections between the brain and our overall well-being.

In her spare time, Ameri enjoys indulging in her passion for reading and writing, constantly expanding her knowledge in the fields of wellness and neuroscience.

Ameri's warm and relatable approach, complete with her scientific expertise, makes her a trusted voice for individuals seeking to enhance their lives through evidence-based practices.

Her book will undoubtedly inspire readers to prioritize self-care, embrace healthier lifestyles, and unlock their fullest potential.

Share Your Thoughts on My Book

Thank you for taking the time to read my book.
If you enjoyed it, I would greatly appreciate if you could leave a review.
I genuinely value each and every review, as they not only help me, but
also provide guidance to other readers.

References

Belujon, P., & Grace, A. A. (2015). Regulation of dopamine system responsivity and its adaptive and pathological response to stress. *Proceedings of the Royal Society B: Biological Sciences, 282*(1805), 20142516. https://doi.org/10.1098/rspb.2014.2516

Belujon, P., & Grace, A. A. (2017). Dopamine system dysregulation in major depressive disorders. *International Journal of Neuropsychopharmacology, 20*(12), 1036–1046. https://doi.org/10.1093/ijnp/pyx056

Berkheiser, K. (2018, August). *12 dopamine supplements to boost your mood.* Healthline; Healthline Media. https://www.healthline.com/nutrition/dopamine-supplements

Berzman, R. (2023, June 7). *16 tips for creating a successful morning routine.* Indeed Career Guide. https://www.indeed.com/career-advice/career-development/morning-success-routine

Budson, A. E. (2021, May 13). *Can mindfulness change your brain?* Harvard Health. https://www.health.harvard.edu/blog/can-mindfulness-change-your-brain-202105132455

Carter, C. (2021, January 26). *How to structure your day to feel less stressed.* Greater Good. https://greatergood.berkeley.edu/article/item/how_to_structure_your_day_to_accomplish_more

Cleveland Clinic. (2022a). *Dopamine deficiency: Symptoms, causes & treatment.* Cleveland Clinic.

https://my.clevelandclinic.org/health/articles/22588-
dopamine-deficiency

Cleveland Clinic. (2022b, March 23). *Dopamine: What it is, function &
symptoms.* Cleveland Clinic.
https://my.clevelandclinic.org/health/articles/22581-
dopamine

Gomes, F. V., & Grace, A. A. (2018). Cortical dopamine dysregulation
in schizophrenia and its link to stress. *Brain, 141*(7), 1897–1899.
https://doi.org/10.1093/brain/awy156

Gorrell, S., Shott, M. E., & Frank, G. K. W. (2022). Associations between
aerobic exercise and dopamine-related reward-processing:
Informing a model of human exercise engagement. *Biological
Psychology, 171,* 108350.
https://doi.org/10.1016/j.biopsycho.2022.108350

Gupta, S. (2023, August 11). *Does a "dopamine detox" actually work? Here's
what a psychiatrist says.* Verywell Mind.
https://www.verywellmind.com/dopamine-detox-7574395

Healthdirect Australia. (2021, November 1). *Dopamine.*
Www.healthdirect.gov.au.
https://www.healthdirect.gov.au/dopamine#:~:text=Having%
20low%20levels%20of%20dopamine

How to do dopamine detox the right way. (n.d.). Www.deprocrastination.co.
https://www.deprocrastination.co/blog/how-to-do-dopamine-
detox-the-right-way

How to dopamine detox? 5 simple tips that you can do. (2022, November 9).
MagnifyMinds. https://magnifymind.com/how-to-dopamine-
detox/

Howes, O. D., McCutcheon, R., Owen, M. J., & Murray, R. M. (2017).
The role of Genes, stress, and dopamine in the development of

schizophrenia. *Biological Psychiatry*, *81*(1), 9–20. https://doi.org/10.1016/j.biopsych.2016.07.014

Juárez Olguín, H., Calderón Guzmán, D., Hernández García, E., & Barragán Mejía, G. (2016). The role of dopamine and its dysfunction as a consequence of oxidative stress. *Oxidative Medicine and Cellular Longevity*, *2016*(1), 1–13. https://doi.org/10.1155/2016/9730467

Julson, E. (2018, May 10). *10 best ways to increase dopamine levels naturally.* Healthline; Healthline Media. https://www.healthline.com/nutrition/how-to-increase-dopamine

Klaus, K., & Pennington, K. (2019). Dopamine and working memory: Genetic variation, stress and implications for mental health. *Processes of Visuospatial Attention and Working Memory*, 369–391. https://doi.org/10.1007/7854_2019_113

Klein, M. O., Battagello, D. S., Cardoso, A. R., Hauser, D. N., Bittencourt, J. C., & Correa, R. G. (2018). Dopamine: Functions, signaling, and association with neurological diseases. *Cellular and Molecular Neurobiology*, *39*(1), 31–59. https://doi.org/10.1007/s10571-018-0632-3

Konkel, L. (2018, August 10). *Dopamine: A neurotransmitter | Everyday Health.* EverydayHealth.com. https://www.everydayhealth.com/dopamine/

Love, T. M. (2014). Oxytocin, motivation and the role of dopamine. *Pharmacology, Biochemistry, and Behavior*, *0*, 49–60. https://doi.org/10.1016/j.pbb.2013.06.011

Low Dopamine Morning Routine for ADHD PAtients: How to boost productivity and mood? (2023, June 21). Www.focusbear.io. https://www.focusbear.io/blog-post/low-dopamine-morning-routine-for-adhd-patients-how-to-boost-productivity-and-mood

Maggie. (2023, February 13). *Useful dopamine detox rules ∗ Simple Girls Life*. Simple Girls Life. https://simplegirlslife.com/blog/useful-dopamine-detox-rules/

Marques, A., Marconcin, P., Werneck, A. O., Ferrari, G., Gouveia, É. R., Kliegel, M., Peralta, M., & Ihle, A. (2021). Bidirectional association between physical activity and dopamine across adulthood—a systematic review. *Brain Sciences, 11*(7), 829. https://doi.org/10.3390/brainsci11070829

The Mid-Atlantic Permanente Medical Group. (2021, December 22). *My doctor online | blogs & news*. Mydoctor.kaiserpermanente.org. https://mydoctor.kaiserpermancnte.org/mas/news/regular-exercise-benefits-both-mind-and-body-a-psychiatrist-explains-1903986

Neophytou, E., Manwell, L. A., & Eikelboom, R. (2019). Effects of excessive screen time on neurodevelopment, learning, memory, mental health, and neurodegeneration: A scoping review. *International Journal of Mental Health and Addiction, 19*(3). https://doi.org/10.1007/s11469-019-00182-2

Ohwovoriole, T. (2022, October 17). *How to increase your dopamine levels naturally*. Verywell Mind. https://www.verywellmind.com/natural-ways-to-increase-your-dopamine-levels-5120223

Pagano, R. (2018, December 21). *Sleep and dopamine*. Sleepline. https://www.sleepline.com/sleep-and-dopamine/

Plumptre, E. (2023, February 14). *What are the signs of low dopamine?* Verywell Mind. https://www.verywellmind.com/common-symptoms-of-low-dopamine-

5120239#:~:text=Low%20dopamine%20symptoms%20can%2
0cause

Powledge, T. M. (2008, September 15). *The dope on dopamine's central role in the Brain's motivation and reward networks.* Scientific American. https://www.scientificamerican.com/article/dopamines-central-role-brains-motivation-reward/

Public Library of Science. (2012, June 19). *The role of dopamine in sleep regulation.* ScienceDaily. https://www.sciencedaily.com/releases/2012/06/1206192257 25.htm

Rhodes, D. (2021, July 7). *10 foods to raise your dopamine levels & make you happy.* EMediHealth. https://www.emedihealth.com/nutrition/dopamine-boosting-foods

Sandoiu, A. (2017, January 1). *Unmotivated to exercise? Dopamine could be to blame.* Www.medicalnewstoday.com. https://www.medicalnewstoday.com/articles/314978

Sittipo, P., Choi, J., Lee, S., & Lee, Y. K. (2022). The function of gut microbiota in immune-related neurological disorders: a review. *Journal of Neuroinflammation, 19*(1). https://doi.org/10.1186/s12974-022-02510-1

Summer. (2022, October 9). *Can low dopamine cause insomnia | Sleepation.* Sleepation. https://sleepation.com/can-low-dopamine-cause-insomnia/

Team Verywell Health. (2023, May 4). *Serotonin vs. Dopamine: What are the differences?* Verywell Health.

https://www.verywellhealth.com/serotonin-vs-dopamine-5194081

Todd, L. (2021, June 30). *Dopamine detox: How does it work?* Www.medicalnewstoday.com. https://www.medicalnewstoday.com/articles/dopamine-detox

Trafton, A. (2020, April 1). *How dopamine drives brain activity.* MIT McGovern Institute. https://mcgovern.mit.edu/2020/04/01/how-dopamine-drives-brain-activity/

University of St. Augustine for Health Sciences. (2019, October 3). *9 Popular time management techniques and tools.* University of St. Augustine for Health Sciences. https://www.usa.edu/blog/time-management-techniques/

Wood-Moen, R. (2018, November 28). *Healthfully.* Healthfully. https://healthfully.com/dopamine-and-stress-response-6069119.html

World Health Organisation. (2017). *Depression and other common mental disorders global health estimates.* https://apps.who.int/iris/bitstream/handle/10665/254610/WHO-MSD-MER-2017.2-eng.pdf

World Health Organization. (2021). *Mental health: neurological disorders.* Who.int. https://www.who.int/news-room/questions-and-answers/item/mental-health-neurological-disorders

World Health Organization. (2022, June 8). *Mental disorders.* World Health Organization. https://www.who.int/news-room/fact-sheets/detail/mental-disorders

Wu, J. C., Maguire, G., Riley, G., Lee, A., Keator, D., Tang, C., Fallon, J., & Najafi, A. (1997). Increased dopamine activity associated with stuttering. *NeuroReport, 8*(3), 767.

https://journals.lww.com/neuroreport/abstract/1997/02100/increased_dopamine_activity_associated_with.37.aspx

Yagishita, S. (2019). Transient and sustained effects of dopamine and serotonin signaling in motivation-related behavior. *Psychiatry and Clinical Neurosciences, 74*(2), 91–98. https://doi.org/10.1111/pcn.12942

Zhang, C., Huang, L., & Xu, M. (2022). Dopamine control of REM sleep and cataplexy. *Neuroscience Bulletin, 38*(12), 1617–1619. https://doi.org/10.1007/s12264-022-00925-7

Printed in Great Britain
by Amazon

37239815R00076